BECOMING
A
PARENT

FAMILY STUDIES TEXT SERIES

Series Editor: RICHARD J. GELLES, *University of Rhode Island*
Series Associate Editor: ALEXA A. ALBERT, *University of Rhode Island*

This series of textbooks is designed to examine topics relevant to a broad view of family studies. The series is aimed primarily at undergraduate students of family sociology and family relations, among others. Individual volumes will be useful to students in psychology, home economics, counseling, human services, social work, and other related fields. Core texts in the series cover such subjects as theory and conceptual design, research methods, family history, cross-cultural perspectives, and life course analysis. Other texts will cover traditional topics, such as dating and mate selection, parenthood, divorce and remarriage, and family power. Topics that have been receiving more recent public attention will also be dealt with, including family violence, later life families, and fatherhood.

Because of their wide range and coverage, Family Studies Texts can be used singly or collectively to supplement a standard text or to replace one. These books will be of interest to both students and professionals in a variety of disciplines.

Volumes in this series:

1. LATER LIFE FAMILIES
   Timothy H. Brubaker

2. INTIMATE VIOLENCE IN FAMILIES
   Richard J. Gelles & Claire Pedrick Cornell

3. BECOMING A PARENT
   Ralph LaRossa

4. FAMILY RESEARCH METHODS
   Brent C. Miller

5. PATHS TO MARRIAGE
   Bernard I. Murstein

Volumes planned for this series:

THEORIES OF FAMILY LIFE, David M. Klein

WORK AND FAMILY LIFE, Patricia Voydanoff

FAMILY POWER, Maximiliane Szinovacz

FAMILY STRESS, Pauline Boss

DIVORCE, Sharon J. Price & Patrick C. McHenry

REMARRIAGE, Marilyn Ihinger-Tallman & Kay Pasley

CONCEPTUAL FRAMEWORKS FOR FAMILY STUDIES,
   Keith Farrington

BECOMING
A
PARENT

Ralph LaRossa

FAMILY STUDIES 3
TEXT SERIES

SAGE PUBLICATIONS
Beverly Hills   London   New Delhi

To Maureen, Brian, and Adam

For information address:

SAGE Publications, Inc.
275 South Beverly Drive
Beverly Hills, California 90212

SAGE Publications India Pvt. Ltd.
M-32 Market
Greater Kailash I
New Delhi 110 048 India

SAGE Publications Ltd
28 Banner Street
London EC1Y 8QE
England

Printed in the United States of America

Library of Congress Cataloging-in-Publication Data

LaRossa, Ralph.
    Becoming a parent.

(Family studies text series; v. 3)
    1. Parenthood. 2. Parenting—United States. 3. Family
—United States. I. Title. II. Series.
HQ755.8.L368 1986   306.8'74   85-30246
ISBN 0-8039-2145-4
ISBN 0-8039-2146-2 (pbk.)

FIRST PRINTING

Contents

Acknowledgments

I WANT TO SAY thanks to the following people for encouraging and/or helping me to write this book: Alexa Albert, Ann Clark, Shirley Frady, Richard Gelles, Toshi Kii, Carol Lavender, Kristin Marsh, Marcia Robinson, Donald Reitzes, Sheryl Silfen, Janie Wolf—and last, but not least, Maureen Mulligan LaRossa, whose love and understanding made all the difference in the world.

CHAPTER
1

On Becoming
a Parent

IN JANUARY MY SON, Brian, will celebrate his birthday; one month later his younger brother, Adam, will celebrate his. It is not hard to understand why people commemorate the day that they were born. On an existential level only death rivals birth in significance. But as important as Brian and Adam's birthdays are to them (now perhaps more for the gifts that they will receive than for anything else), the event itself is not something that they can remember, as they will someday remember the day they got their first two-wheelers or the day they started high school. Of course, they have been, or will be, told about when they came into the world, but being told about what happened on a given day and personally experiencing that day are not the same thing.

Two people who were present at the boys' births and who definitely will be spending parts of both days reminiscing are myself and my wife, Maureen. Our sons' birthdays are memorable to us because they are the anniversaries of when we became parents.

Which brings me to the point of this book. In the pages that follow, I will relate not what it is like to be born but what it is like to give birth. In other words, I intend to talk not about what it means to become a person but about what it means to become a parent.

Becoming a parent has been described as "a set of apparent contradictions" (Hoffman and Manis, 1978: 211). On the one hand, having a baby is enormously satisfying. On the other hand, parenthood involves a lot of work and can be the source of a tremendous amount of frustration and pain, both physical and psychological. Speaking for myself, Adam and Brian are two of the best things that ever happened to me. But caring for them—and trying to do it "right"—is the toughest job I have ever encountered. Thus, in some respects this book is my story; and, because most people eventually become parents, it probably is (or will be) your story, too.

THE SOCIAL REALITY
OF BECOMING A PARENT

Humans, by nature, reside in a social as well as physical universe and, in many ways, are products of the social reality surrounding them and of which they are a part. By *social reality* I mean "the world of cultural objects and social institutions into which we are all born, within which we have to find our bearings, and with which we have to come to terms" (Schutz, 1971: 53). I am referring specifically to a society's goals, values, beliefs, and norms, as well as the patterns of interpersonal relations that develop from and reinforce these goals, values, beliefs, and norms.

When a dog or cat, or any other animal for that matter, gives birth, it basically has a biological tie to its offspring and is instinctually programmed to care for that offspring in one way or another. By contrast, when a human being gives birth, the social rather than biological tie with the baby is paramount, and how that child is cared for is largely a function of "the world of cultural objects and social institutions" in which the parent and child reside.

Also, at the human level becoming a parent begins not at birth nor even at the onset of pregnancy but at the moment a person decides to have a child. The reason is simple: because, among humans, the transition to parenthood is viewed as a solemn social act (in all known societies birth and parenthood are treated with great reverence and marked with much fanfare), the decision to become a parent is considered a significant step in its own right.

Finally, because of the goals, values, beliefs, and norms associated with having children, people who become parents are perceived differently and treated differently by almost everyone they meet. Parents also perceive themselves differently and act differently than do nonparents. Thus, the transition to parenthood is a transition to a new social status and, correspondingly, a new network of relationships.

THE SOCIAL CONSTRUCTION
OF PARENTHOOD

No theoretical issue intrigues sociologists more than trying to explain how it is possible "that history and society are made by constant and more or less purposeful individual action *and* that individual action, however purposeful, is made by history and society" (Abrams, 1982: xiii).[1] In other words, one cannot deny that norms, values, beliefs, and the like are *made by people*, yet at the same time one cannot deny that these very things also *make people what they are*.

How does the world that we create turn around and create us? This question is necessarily at the core of any discussion of what social reality is, whether it be the social reality of international relations, the social reality of dating and courtship, or—with respect to this book—the social reality of parenthood. Answering the question as it applies to parenthood requires an understanding of three closely linked axioms.

Axiom 1 is that parenthood is a social institution. Axiom 2 is that parental behavior is a product of socialization and internalization. Axiom 3 is that the social institution of parenthood is a human construction (Berger and Luckmann, 1966).

Axiom 1: Parenthood Is
a Social Institution

The *Oxford English Dictionary* defines *parenthood* as "the state or position of a parent" (1970: 475). This definition, however, is only partially correct, for besides being a social position parenthood is also a social institution.

Normally, when people think of institutions they think of bureaucracies, such as hospitals and universities. But from a sociological point of view, an *institution* is a system of values, beliefs, norms, and behaviors that develop around basic social goals or needs (see Eshleman and Cashion, 1985). Thus, parenthood is an institution in the sense that it is a complex of values, beliefs, norms, and behaviors centered on two very important needs—the need to procreate (assuming people want their society to have a future) and the need to care for the young.

Every institution has four characteristics: externality, opaqueness, coerciveness, and legitimacy (Berger and Berger, 1972).[2] If parenthood is a social institution, it must also exhibit these characteristics. Let us see if it does.

Externality: Social institutions are experienced as realities external to humans; they are seen as things that are "out there," hovering above and beyond us.

This certainly seems to be how parenthood is viewed. Consider again the fact that the dictionary defines parenthood as "the state or position of a parent." What is significant about this definition is that it clearly disassociates the reality of parenthood from the people who call themselves parents. Parenthood is the state or position of parents, *not* the parents themselves. Moreover, if we follow the dictionary's logic, we see that parenthood is a reality that may be experienced by parents and nonparents alike. In other words, even people who are unwilling or unable to be parents can experience parenthood in the sense that they can talk about it and evaluate it.

Opaqueness: Social institutions also are experienced as opaque realities. To say that something is opaque is to say that it is hard to understand. Thus, social institutions are experienced as entities that require effort to comprehend.

One need only visit a bookstore to discover that parenthood generally is perceived as a veritable black box. Every year there is a spate of books claiming to solve the mysteries of parenthood, but little evidence to suggest that one method is necessarily better than the next. The fact is that the publishing industry simply is giving parents what they hunger for: answers. And it is making a lot of money in the process. Benjamin Spock's how-to book, *Baby and Child Care*, first published in 1945 and now in its fifth edition, has sold over 30 million copies and is still going strong (Leo and Kalb, 1985).

Coerciveness: The third essential characteristic of social institutions is that they have coercive power, which is to say that people frequently feel that they are forced to follow institutional dictates. Typically, this feeling of powerlessness remains in the recesses of people's minds until they push for change. It is then that they become aware of the prisonlike hold that institutions have on us.

You may, for instance, assume that having children is a matter of personal choice, and as long as you choose to have at least two children you may not question this assumption. But if you decide to remain child-free or have only one child, you will quickly become aware of the pronatalistic (probirth, profertility) pressures surrounding you.

During the early 1970s, a woman by the name of Ellen Peck believed that the pronatalistic pressures were so strong and so offensive that she wrote a book about her experiences (entitled *The Baby Trap*) and helped found an organization devoted to promoting the child-free alternative (the National Organization for Non-Parents, now called the National Alliance for Optional Parenthood). Later on, she wrote another book (entitled *The Joy of the Only Child*) in which she discussed how one-child families are subject to discrimination.

Attitudes certainly have changed since Peck chose to air her grievances and perhaps, in part, because she decided to take a stand; it has become more acceptable for people to opt for nonparenthood or to stop after one child. But the two- or more children family is still viewed as the norm in this country, and people who deviate from that norm are likely to feel some pressure to conform (Hawke and Knox, 1977; Veevers, 1980).

One more thing: The coercive power of the institution of parenthood does not necessarily involve pressures to have two children. This just happens to be the case in the United States. China, for example, recently enacted a one-couple-one-child policy (Huang, 1982), which sometimes requires that women display their sanitary napkins on demand to show that they are not pregnant and submit to abortions if they conceive after having had one child (Henslin, 1985). What makes matters even worse is that because of the strong preference in China for male children, thousands of female babies are being murdered by their own families to "make room" for sons (Light, 1985).

Legitimacy: Finally, social institutions have legitimacy. People often feel that the institutional constraints placed upon them are moral, good, right, and so on, and correspondingly view others who deviate as immoral, bad, wrong, and so on.

Few institutions are imbued with as much legitimacy as parenthood. Many major religions, in fact, interpret parenthood as a sacred responsibility. And in this society and most others being a parent is viewed as a sign that one is sexually competent, mentally alert, and socially mature (Veevers, 1973). It is not hard, therefore, to understand why people who choose not to have children and people who are unable to have children traditionally have been ridiculed and ostracized.

Axiom 2: Parental Behavior Is a Product of Socialization and Internalization

Linking the social institution of parenthood with individual parents (and nonparents) requires that we combine two levels of analysis. Social institutions such as parenthood are *macro-* (large-scale) phenomena, and individual behaviors are *micro-* (small-scale) phenomena.

Situated at the junction of these two levels are what are called roles. *Roles* are shared norms (agreed upon do's and don'ts) associated with social positions. Thus, the shared norms associated with the father position constitute the father role, and the shared norms associated with the mother position constitute the mother role.

Becoming a parent in large part is the result of having been taught to play a variety of parental roles, including not only the father or mother role but also, depending on the circumstances, the expectant parent role, the new parent role, the full-time parent role, the employed parent role, and so on. The process by which these roles are learned is known as *socialization*.

Every role is tied to one or more social institutions. For example, the parental roles just mentioned are tied to the institution of parenthood as well as to the institution of the family. Hence, when people are socialized to play one parental role or another, they are beginning to feel the effect that the institution of parenthood has on their personal lives. Actually, the effect is more pronounced than the word *socialization* suggests, for we do not simply learn roles, we *internalize* roles. We absorb the roles we play to such a degree that our sense of who we are (our identities) and our sense of right and wrong (our consciences) are very much a product of our role-playing activities. Thus, an American woman who has a child probably not only behaves like a mother should in this society (that is, she does what people expect someone *in her position* to do), but also transforms her view of herself and her world.

Parental socialization and internalization begin early in life. When you were a child it is likely that you played house and equally likely that the game itself was organized along fairly traditional lines, with the boys playing daddies and the girls playing mommies. If you have a kid brother and/or sister you also may have had the opportunity to play the role of surrogate parent—feeding, cleaning, and monitoring a younger sibling when your parents were out. And as a teenager you may have been asked to baby-sit and again been thrust into a position in which you had to "act like" a parent. All of these are preparatory socialization experiences that can have a bearing on an individual's decision to become a parent and on the kind of parent (or nonparent) he or she is likely to be.

As significant as child socialization is, by no means is it the only socialization experience that we have, and by no means is it sufficient to understand how and why people act the way that they do. Upon becoming adults we are immersed in the institution of parenthood and are bombarded with messages about the meaning of parenthood and about what is and what is not proper parental conduct.

The idea that parenthood "belongs" to women, for instance, is one message that we continue to receive long after we have stopped playing house. I remember receiving the 1979 Father's Day issue of *American Baby* (a magazine for expectant and new parents that is free for the asking) when my son Brian was about five months old. Although fathers were supposed to be "the center of attention" in this special issue, few of the advertisements in the magazine depicted men being fathers. Also, the magazine had a regular column entitled "Mart for *Mothers* and Baby," describing a variety of new baby products that, theoretically at least, would be of interest to both moms and dads. (The issue did, however, have an article on baby items apparently endorsed by a small sample of fathers.) Finally, the special Father's Day issue was addressed, as were all the other issues that we had received, to *Mrs.* R. LaRossa. In spite of its good intentions (according to the magazine's editor, "Sharing responsibility for child raising is what fatherhood is all about today"), this issue of *American Baby* reinforced the belief that men are second-class citizens when it comes to taking care of children. And to the extent that people are affected by what they read, *American Baby* plays some part in the socialization to parenthood.

Although magazines, newspapers, television, and the like are significant shapers (and reflections) of public opinion about parenthood, most adult socialization experiences relating to parenthood take place during face-to-face encounters. A woman is told by her parents that she is neglecting her baby by continuing to work outside the home.

A man is warned by his boss that he will jeopardize his job if he continues to define Saturdays as family days rather than company days. These experiences, too, have the effect of socializing adults into "the way" of parenthood in this society.

Axiom 3: Parenthood
Is a Human Construction

Some people believe that the institution of parenthood is created *for us* by nonhuman forces (for example, nature) and that individual actions are simply products of the institution itself. But the truth is that the institution of parenthood and parental behavior are reciprocally related: Parenthood shapes us and we, in turn, shape parenthood.

How does the institution-construction process work? The key is *communication*, both verbal and nonverbal. For example, when a grandfather and grandmother tell their daughter that, in their opinion, she is neglecting her son (their grandchild) by being employed, not only are they trying to teach their daughter something, they are also promoting the notion that a mother's place is in the home. If, as a result of what they say (social pressure), the daughter is moved to quit her job and indicates to all concerned (her parents, her son, her husband, her boss, her friends, and so on) that she believes she was neglecting her child, she too is promoting the notion that a mother's place is in the home. And if this sequence of communications happens in enough families, the notion that a woman's place is in the home has a good chance of becoming a constituent part of the social institution of parenthood.

Suppose, however, that the daughter rejects her parents' argument. Suppose she says that she intends to continue to work because her job makes her happy, and she believes that she is a better mother because she is happy. And suppose she is so committed to this view that she becomes a working-mother's advocate, someone dedicated to extolling the virtues of combining a career and motherhood. Under the circumstances she would not be promoting the notion that a woman's place is in the home; if anything, she would be promoting the opposite. Now suppose a significant percentage of women felt and acted the same way. What do you think would happen? The social institution of parenthood would be transformed.

You may or may not know it, but such a transformation already has taken place. Whereas in the early 1900s it was typically considered unacceptable for mothers to be employed, today with over 60% of married women in the United States working outside the home, it has become, if not totally acceptable, at least tolerated; and for many career women the work-family combination is not simply tolerated but embraced.

By the way, not everyone has an equal voice in the institution-construction process. If you are interested in changing the social institution of parenthood (or interested in maintaining the status quo), it helps to have not only a significant number of people on your side but also a number of significant people (that is, powerful people) speaking on your behalf. In other words, the communication mechanisms supporting institutional realities are intimately tied to power structures at both the micro- and macro-levels, which is why sociologists often depict the institution-construction process as a political game in which various interest groups (for example, Democrats, Republicans, feminists, the Moral Majority) compete to have their views become part of the mainstream.

HISTORY AND PARENTHOOD

Parenthood is a social institution. Parental behavior is a product of socialization and internalization. Parenthood is a human construction. Although it is possible, grammatically and analytically, to talk about one axiom, then another, then the third, it is impossible experientially to separate the three. Parenthood as a social institution is dependent for its existence on human activity, in particular communication. Parental behavior, at least among humans, requires that there be a parental institution. And the institution-construction process is inexorably tied to the processes of socialization and internalization.

It is important to emphasize that we are talking about a process that occurs *over time*. If you recall, the theoretical issue that, more than any other, seems to intrigue sociologists and the issue that led to my discussion of the social construction of parenthood in the first place is the question of how society *and history* are connected to individual action. Thus, the institution of parenthood at Time 1 influences parental socialization and internalization at Time 2, which, in turn, influences the human construction of parenthood at Time 3.

I really cannot stress enough how important it is not to ignore the historical dimension, for the fact is that a historical perspective is indispensible not only to the study of the social construction of parenthood but to the study of the social construction of anything.

The two-sidedness of society, the fact that social action is both something we choose to do and something we have to do, is inseparably bound up with the further fact that whatever reality society has is an historical reality, a reality in time. When we refer to the two-sidedness of society we are referring to the ways in which, in time, actions become institutions and institutions are in turn changed by actions. . . . In both its aspects, then, the social world is essentially historical [Abrams, 1982: 2-3].

I should note also that by "a historical perspective" I do not mean exclusively a macro-perspective. Certainly it is important to be sensitive to large-scale transformations that may take decades to develop (for example, the Industrial Revolution), but these are not the only transitions that play a role in the social-construction process. Equally important are the micro-transformations that unfold over much shorter periods of time.

History, the interaction of structure and action, is not . . . something that happens only on the large stage of whole societies or civilizations. It also occurs in prisons, factories and schools, in families, firms and friendships. Any relationship that persists in time has a history if we choose to think of it in those terms; action in even the most restricted setting can be treated historically because it has a history. The state of childhood is also the process of growing up. The condition of being ill is also the process of becoming cured. And even in these small-scale social settings teasing out historical processes, the sociology of *becoming*, is for the sociologist the best way of discovering the real relationship of structure and action, the structural conditioning of action and the effects of action on structure [Abrams, 1982: 6-7].

Thus, the study of what it means to become a parent is more than the study of how large-scale events have shaped and continue to shape the experience of having and rearing a child; it is also the study of how micro-events—specifically, the day-in-and-day-out dynamics of becoming a parent—have shaped and continue to shape the social reality of parenthood.

BIOLOGY AND PARENTHOOD

Up to now I have discussed becoming a parent without reference to two important issues: (1) For the present parenthood is tied to a reproductive process that is based upon anatomical differences between men and women (advances in biotechnology eventually may alter how babies are made); and (2) there is a possibility that sex dimorphism (that is, the separation of men and women into different morphologic and psychologic forms) partially explains why, almost always, women are primarily responsible for infant care.

As far as the first issue is concerned, the fact that only women can be physically pregnant undoubtedly results in different psychosocial experiences for expectant fathers and mothers. To take but one example, mothers-to-be more often think about the fetus, wonder how it is developing, and so on, than do fathers-to-be (Stainton, 1985). Of course, this is hardly surprising; after all, the babies are growing *inside of the mothers* and not their husbands. I am not denying that social factors also contribute to differences in how men and women experience pregnancy. I am simply noting that, when it comes to biological events such as pregnancy and birth, biological *and* social factors must be taken into account.

The second of the two issues—that sex dimorphism may play a part in the division of infant care—is more complex and, right now, extremely controversial. Some scholars believe that biologically based gender differences—specifically, chromosomal, hormonal, and neural differences between males and females—are responsible for differences in the quantity and quality of infant fathering and mothering.

You might think that biologists would be the only ones advocating this view, but the truth is that at present the leading proponent of this theory is a sociologist. Alice Rossi, who is a former president of the American Sociological Association (ASA), argues that social scientists are making a serious mistake by refusing to integrate biological and social constructs (see Rossi, 1977, 1984).

Rossi has a point. For a long time now social scientists have pretended that biological factors simply do not matter and thus are not worthy of discussion. Not all social scientists have been equally blind to biology. Anthropologists and psychologists never excluded anatomy and physiology from their respective disciplines (hence, the existence of courses and texts on physical anthropology and physiological psychology). No, for the most part it is the academic sociologists (that is, sociology Ph.D.s) to whom Rossi is speaking and who seem to be the most bothered by what Rossi has to say.

What exactly is Rossi saying? Basically, she is proposing that one reason that mothers are primarily responsible for infant care is that "biological predispositions" make it "easier" for women to care for babies. For example, in her ASA presidential address she argues as follows:

> Viewed as a composite profile, there is some predisposition in the female to be responsive to people and sounds, an edge in receiving, interpreting and giving back communication. Males have an edge on finer differentiation of the physical world through better spatial visualization and physical object manipulation. The female combination of sensitivity to sound and face and rapid processing of peripheral information implies a quicker judgement of emotional nuance, a profile that carries a put-down tone when labelled "female intuition." It also suggests an easier connection between feelings and their expression in words among women. Spatial perception, good gross motor control, visual acuity, and a more rigid division between emotional and cognitive responsivity combine in a counterpart profile of the male. . . . When these gender differences are viewed in connection with caring for a nonverbal, fragile infant, then women have a head start in easier reading of an infant's facial expressions, smoothness of body motions, greater ease in handling a tiny creature with tactile gentleness, and in soothing through a high, soft, rhythmic use of the voice. By contrast, men have tendencies more congenial to interaction with an older child, with whom rough-and-tumble physical play, physical coordination, teaching of object coordination are easier and more congenial [Rossi, 1984: 13].

Rossi goes on to say that the predispositions that she describes are "general tendencies" that may be "exaggerated" or "reversed" through sex-differentiated socialization practices. Thus, the predispositions are not "biologically immutable or invariant across individuals or cultures" (Rossi, 1984: 13).

The fact that Rossi believes that biological tendencies can be modified is highly significant. Rossi is not arguing that biological and social factors are in competition with one another; she is not resurrecting the ill-conceived nature versus nurture (or heredity versus environment) debate. Rather, she is saying that biological and social factors *interact with one another.*

Biological processes unfold in a cultural context, and are themselves malleable, not stable and inevitable. So too, cultural processes take place within and through the biological organism; they do not take place in a biological vacuum [Rossi, 1984: 10].

Whether Rossi is correct in attributing so much importance to sex dimorphism is open to question (see, for example, Gross et al., 1979; Altman et al., 1984). I, for one, happen to believe that the evidence she cites is not enough to support her view, and that she gives too little attention to the role that power and economics play in the division of infant care. However, I do think that when it comes to understanding parenthood, it is imperative that we strive to develop theories that synthesize biological and social factors. Rossi may have overcompensated in her eagerness to "bring biology back in," but at least she made a step in the right (general) direction.

Although a biosocial perspective on parenthood will not be presented in this volume—to do so would require, among other things, an extensive discussion of human physiology and anatomy and a critical review of the ethological evidence—the interaction between biological and social factors will not be ignored either. For example, the biology of conception and pregnancy will be discussed within a social context, and the social reality of birth will be tied to the physical stages of labor, parturition, and delivery. Basically, however, this is a book on the *sociology* of becoming a parent and, as such, focuses primarily on the historical relationship between society on the one hand and the thoughts, feelings, and actions of prospective and new parents on the other.

CONCLUSION

The object of this family studies text is to describe what it means to become a parent, beginning with a discussion of how people decide to have a child and concluding with a discussion of what happens to new parents during the first twelve months or so of their baby's life.

The theme of the book is that besides being a biological process, becoming a parent is a social act. Thus, I will endeavor to show how the social institution of parenthood (as defined in this chapter) shapes the behavior of prospective and new parents and, conversely, how the behavior of prospective and new parents shapes the social institution of parenthood.

I recommend that as you read the book you keep in mind the three axioms introduced in this chapter: namely, that (1) parenthood is a social institution, (2) parental behavior is a product of socialization and internalization, and (3) parenthood is a human construction. Also, try not to lose sight of the fact that these three axioms exist in a historical context, that they represent three phases in a process that, at both macro- and micro-levels, occurs over time.

REVIEW QUESTIONS

(1) How is parenthood a social institution, and how do the four characteristics embodied in every institution (externality, opaqueness, coerciveness, and legitimacy) manifest themselves in the social institution of parenthood?

(2) How is parental behavior a product of child socialization and internalization? How is it a product of adult socialization and internalization?

(3) What part do communication and power play in constructing the social institution of parenthood?

(4) Why is a historical perspective essential to the study of becoming a parent?

(5) Why is a biological perspective essential to the study of becoming a parent?

SUGGESTED ASSIGNMENTS

(1) Select four people—a father, a mother, a childless male, and a childless female—and ask them what they think about "parenthood in America."

(2) Locate six newspaper or magazine articles that deal with becoming a parent (that is, articles on pregnancy, birth, and so on) and identify the explicit and implicit messages that each contains about the "proper" way to have a child.

(3) Review your life and try to determine how your attitude toward parenthood has been shaped by your socialization experiences, both as a child and as an adult.

NOTES

1. Here and throughout this book I use the term *sociologists* to refer to people who study social reality. I am not referring only to people with advanced degrees in sociology, for anyone may choose to study the social world in which we live. Indeed, there are novelists, playwrights, journalists, anthropologists, psychologists, and historians whose work constitutes some of the best sociology around. It also follows that when I use the term *sociology* I am referring not simply to what sociology Ph.D.s do but to a perspective (soon to be described) that may be used by anyone (see Mills, 1959: 19).

2. Sociologists Brigette and Peter Berger would say that there is another characteristic that social institutions have: historicity (Berger and Berger, 1972). But I prefer not to limit history to the institutional sphere and will use the historical dimension to tie the three axioms together, as you will soon see.

CHAPTER
2

Fertility Rates
and Fertility
Decision Making

THERE WERE APPROXIMATELY 3.7 million births in the United States last year, which translates into about 1,000 births per day, or one birth every 8.5 seconds (National Center for Health Statistics, 1985).

Each of these births is the product of a series of decisions. Children do not just "happen." They must be conceived and given the opportunity to grow and develop inside a woman's uterus. Thus, the fact that you were born means that your parents decided on some level of consciousness to (1) conceive you and (2) not abort you.

The purpose of this chapter is twofold. First, I will paint a demographic picture of the parent population in the United States and discuss how and why fertility rates have changed over the past thirty years and how and why they are likely to change in the future. Second, I will describe the key factors involved in making the decision to have a child. My goal essentially is to provide both a panorama and an in-depth portrait of the first stages in the process of becoming a parent.

FERTILITY RATES
IN THE UNITED STATES

The number of children that the average woman is capable of bearing is called the *fecundity rate*, and the number of children that the average woman actually bears is called the *fertility rate*.[1] Theoretically, it is possible for a woman to have as many as twenty children, if she starts conceiving soon after she begins to menstruate and continues in rapid succession through menopause. Because of health and social factors, however, the number of children actually born is much lower (Robertson, 1981: 510). For example, most women in the United States today give birth to two children, whereas back in the 1930s most women in the United States gave birth to three or four children. And although today it is rare to find a woman who has given birth to five or more children, one hundred years ago the proportion of women in this category was fairly high—about 30% (Thornton and Freedman, 1983: 14). This is not to say that one-third of all families during the late 1800s had five or more children, for although the fertility rate was high, so was the percentage of children who did not survive infancy (Dally, 1982: 25-43).

Fertility Control:
Contraception and Abortion

The two principal means of controlling (that is, reducing and timing) fertility are contraception and abortion. Contraception prevents conception or impregnation. Abortion prevents birth.

Contraception is not a new idea. On the contrary, it is an age-old practice.

Contraception . . . is a social practice of much greater historical antiquity, greater cultural and geographical universality than commonly supposed even by medical and social historians. Contraception has existed in some form throughout the entire range of social evolution, that is, for at least several thousand years. The *desire for*, as distinct from the *achievement of*, reliable contraception has been characteristic of many societies widely removed in time and place. Moreover, this desire for controlled reproduction characterizes even those societies dominated by mores and religious codes demanding that people "increase and multiply" [Himes, 1970: xii].

What kinds of contraceptive techniques have been employed throughout history? Preliterate societies relied on magic, and the early Egyptians and Greeks, who had some understanding of the anatomy of reproduction, mainly used *coitus interruptus* (withdrawal), vaginal blocks, and potions (Himes, 1970). Fifty years ago in this country the most popular methods of contraception were withdrawal, condoms, and douches (Kopp, 1934). Today, the most popular methods used by women in the United States between the ages of 15 and 44—the "childbearing years," according to the U.S. Census—are sterilization (32%—that is, 19% of the women in this age category have had tubal ligations and 13% of the women in this age category have male partners who have had vasectomies), pills (27%), condoms (12%), intrauterine devices (6%), diaphragms (5%), spermicides (4%), withdrawal (3%), and rhythm (2%). The most popular contraceptive methods among women under 30, on the other hand, are pills (43%) and condoms (15%) (Forrest and Henshaw, 1983: 163).

Abortion also has been used throughout history to control fertility. Indeed, the main form of conscious "birth control" in primitive societies was abortion (Himes, 1970: 4). The oldest medical texts include references to abortifacients (for example, injecting mercury into the uterus or tearing the uterine wall with a sharp object). And although today there are strict laws that prescribe when an abortion can and cannot be carried out, there apparently were few, if any, sanctions against abortion in ancient times (Krannich, 1980).

As for the United States,

> The first law dealing specifically with the legal status of abortion . . . was passed in 1821 by the General Assembly of Connecticut. It restricted the administration of a "noxious or destructive substance . . . to any woman then quick with child" [i.e., to any woman who was far enough along in her pregnancy to feel the fetus move]. . . . Surgical abortion before quickening was first prohibited by a section of the New York Revised Statutes of 1829 (enacted in 1828), which also contained an express therapeutic exception, justifying abortion "if necessary to preserve the life of the mother." . . . A review of documents contemporary with the passage of the New York State legislation suggests that the primary concern at the time was not with the unquickened fetus but with protecting the life and health of women with unwanted pregnancies from damage by abortion. . . . In most hospitals [then] one operation in three ended in death [David, 1981: 5-6].

In 1967, Colorado liberalized its laws on abortion, allowing the procedure to be performed not only to save the life of the mother but also in the event of rape, incest, or congenital deformities in the fetus. In 1970, Alaska, Hawaii, New York, and Washington went even further and removed all legal controls on abortions performed during the first three months of pregnancy (Hodgson and Ward, 1981: 519).

In 1973, the U.S. Supreme Court issued two landmark rulings that expanded the parameters dictating when an abortion could be legally performed. The first, *Roe v. Wade,* ruled that up until the time that a fetus was "viable" (that is, potentially able to live outside the mother's womb, with or without artificial aid), the abortion decision was a private matter between a woman and her physician. The Court deliberately did not fix viability at any specific point in the pregnancy, saying that usually it occurred around 28 weeks but could occur as early as 24 weeks. After "viability," the abortion decision was to be proscribed by federal, state, and local governments. Basically, the Court argued that abortions could not be performed after this point "except where it is necessary, in appropriate medical judgment, for the preservation of the life or health of the mother." Who decides if the mother's life or health is at stake? This is where the second ruling comes into play. In the companion case, *Doe v. Bolton,* the Court ruled that a physician could take into account an array of factors—physical, emotional, psychological, familial, chronological—to determine the threat to a woman's life (Lucas and Miller, 1981). It is these two decisions that basically shape abortion policy in the United States today, and it is these two decisions that are at the heart of the battle currently raging between pro- and antiabortion forces (see Luker, 1984).

Compiling accurate statistics on the number of abortions performed is difficult because "no reliable method exists to estimate the number of illegal abortions, whether performed by doctors, midwives, or other practitioners, nor of abortions induced by the pregnant women themselves" (Tietze and Lewit, 1981: 42). However, if we look only at legal abortions, it appears that the number of abortions carried out in the United States since the two Supreme Court rulings has more than doubled: In 1973, there were about 750,000 abortions performed; and in 1982, there were about 1.6 million. It is estimated that now more than one-fourth of all pregnancies end in abortion (Beck et al., 1985; also see Henshaw and O'Reilly, 1983).

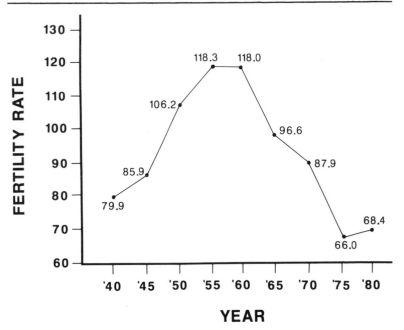

SOURCES: *Vital Statistics Rates in the United States 1940-1960; Statistical Abstracts of the United States 1976; Statistical Abstracts of the United States 1985.*

Figure 2.1   Births Per 1,000 Women, 15-44 Years Old, 1940-1980

The Fertility Rate from
World War II to the Present

A picture of how the fertility rate in the United States has changed since World War II is provided in Figure 2.1. Note the sharp increase in the number of births between 1945 and 1955. This increase generally is known as the postwar "baby boom." The postwar period was a time of both strong familistic values and a healthy economy, and sociologists speculate that the combination of the two contributed to the increased number of births (Cherlin, 1981).

As you can see, the fertility rate dropped considerably between 1960 and 1975. This decline—sometimes referred to as the "baby bust"—has been attributed to several factors. First, more and more women have been going to college and graduate school, and the more education women have, the fewer children they generally bear. Second, in part because of their increased interest in getting an education, women have been marrying later. Women who postpone marriage until after they are 25 generally have fewer children. Third, more women are working outside the home. In some cases it is for financial reasons—to help the family make ends meet. In other cases it is because of a strong commitment to a career and the rewards that it brings. Whatever their reasons for working outside the home, however, women who are employed generally have fewer children than women who are not employed. (I will have more to say about this in a moment.) Finally, the availability of more effective contraceptives has probably contributed to the decrease in the fertility rate (Melville, 1983: 354-355).

Since 1975, the fertility rate has climbed somewhat, and sociologists are hard pressed to explain why. Some, pointing out that the most rapid increase occurred among women aged 25 to 34 who were having their first child, suggest that the upswing is due to women having the children that they had delayed having earlier (Scanzoni and Scanzoni, 1981: 554). There is a definite trend toward delaying parenthood (Wilkie, 1981), but whether this accounts for the slight increase is open to question. Others believe that we are on the brink of another baby boom, and they suggest that the renewed interest in family issues will have the kind of effect evidenced after World War II (Reed, 1982). Although "anything is bound to happen," the fertility rate is not likely to increase to the degree that it did between 1945 and 1955. In fact, it may ultimately decrease. At least that is what the Census Bureau thinks will happen. The U.S. government projects that between 1980 and 2000 the fertility rate will steadily decline to 61.4 (Wetrogan, 1983).

The Fertility Rate in
Selected Age and Socioeconomic Groups

Table 2.1 offers an overview of how the fertility rate in 1980 varied by age, education, labor force status, and family income. The reason the table excludes the first three "childbearing years" (that is, 15 to 17) is because the data are based not on vital statistics reports published by the National Center for Health Statistics but on a national probability sample of approximately 36,000 women. The advantage of relying on a survey rather than birth certificates is that in a survey you can gather information about variables besides race and age (O'Connell and Rogers, 1982).

TABLE 2.1

Number of First and Subsequent Births Per 1,000 Women
by Age, Education, Labor Force Status, and Family Income

	First Births			All Births		
	18-44	*18-29*	*30-44*	*18-44*	*18-29*	*30-44*
Education						
<High school graduate	28.1	54.1	2.5	91.9	150.9	34.0
High school graduate	30.2	54.0	3.5	71.5	111.3	27.1
1-3 years college	25.2	37.0	8.0	58.4	72.5	37.5
4 years college	29.4	44.7	14.4	65.9	71.3	61.1
⩾5 years college	25.4	40.0	18.0	52.1	63.0	46.1
Labor Force Status						
In labor force	19.7	32.7	4.4	40.9	58.1	20.7
employed	18.2	31.0	4.2	37.4	53.1	20.2
full time	16.7	28.2	3.9	33.6	47.2	18.7
part time	23.0	39.3	4.9	48.9	71.2	24.7
looking for work	34.6	45.3	7.4	75.0	94.8	28.3
Not in labor force	45.6	82.9	9.6	130.1	202.0	61.1
Family Income						
<$5,000	32.5	47.7	3.1	94.3	126.2	34.1
$5,000-9,999	34.4	53.2	4.7	86.8	118.0	36.2
$10,000-14,999	34.2	54.5	5.8	83.9	120.7	32.5
$15,000-19,999	26.6	46.3	5.0	77.1	115.3	35.8
$20,000-24,999	33.5	61.9	7.1	69.8	104.9	37.4
⩾$25,000	19.7	34.9	8.3	48.5	63.5	37.1
All Women	28.5	48.6	6.3	71.1	103.7	35.4

SOURCE: "Differential fertility in the United States: 1976-1980," by Martin O'Connell and Carolyn C. Rogers. Reprinted and adapted with permission from *Family
Planning Perspectives,* Volume 14, Number 5, 1982.

Looking at the table we can see that most births occurred among
women who were under 30. However, the differences between the 18 to
29 group and the 30 to 44 group varied by several of the characteristics
listed. For example, college-educated women were more likely than
other women to have children while in their 30s, and especially more
likely to have their *first* child while in their 30s. A similar relationship
exists for family income. Women in families with an income of at least
$25,000 were more likely than other women to have children while in
their 30s and especially more likely to have their *first* child while in
their 30s.

We see also that, as noted earlier, the relationship between labor-
force participation and fertility is very strong. The fertility rate in 1980

for women in the labor force (which includes both the employed and those looking for work) was 40.9, whereas the rate for women not in the labor force (full-time homemakers) was 130.1. Bear in mind that the connection between labor-force participation and fertility is reciprocal. Working outside the home may incline a woman to have fewer children, but being a full-time homemaker also could reflect a stronger commitment to being a mother, which in turn could mean feeling comfortable with having more children than other people might have (Sweet, 1982).

FERTILITY DECISION MAKING

The Big Decision

"The most fateful decision of your life" is how one book describes it (Whelan, 1975). "The most important choice of your life" says another (Bombardieri, 1981). The decision or choice to which these books refer is whether to become a parent.

Why is the decision to become a parent so significant? There are several reasons. First, it is a decision that for all practical purposes is irrevocable. You can decide to take a course and then withdraw if the course proves disappointing. You can buy a house and later sell it if for some reason it loses its appeal. And you can marry your childhood sweetheart and then turn around and get a divorce. But, except in the case of giving up your child for adoption or abandoning him or her on somebody's doorstep, once you become a parent you *stay* a parent (Rossi, 1968).

There is also the financial cost of having children. A recent study concluded that,

> an average, two parent family with no previous children and [husband] aged twenty five in 1980 can expect to spend a total of $214,956 (1982 dollars, undiscounted) to raise a son born in 1980 from birth to age twenty-two, assuming that the son is not expected to attend a residential private college [Olson, 1983: 55].

This is the cost for one child. Raising two children would cost $357,171, and raising three children would cost $475,046! Also, note

TABLE 2.2
Lifetime Costs (1982 dollars) of Having Male Children,
Two Parents, Average Income

	One Child	Two Children	Three Children
Food at home	69,584.51	113,060.96	150,858.54
Housing	65,006.70	109,417.72	145,370.62
Clothing	8,958.81	15,088.14	20,044.79
Transportation	29,254.89	47,567.14	63,538.02
Health	14,973.44	25,521.07	33,672.51
Other	27,177.63	46,516.41	61,561.30
Total	$214,955.98	$357,171.44	$475,045.78

SOURCE: Reprinted by permission of the publisher, from *Costs of Children* by
Lawrence Olson (Lexington, MA: D. C. Heath and Company). Copyright 1983, D. C.
Heath and Company.
NOTE: Costs of residential private college are not included.

that these are the costs for male children. Raising female children is
even more expensive.

The reason that raising two or three children is not double or triple
the cost of raising one child is that some possessions, such as a
television or hi-fi system, can be shared by children; also, second and
third children often receive hand-me-downs from their older brothers
and sisters. As to why raising female children is more expensive than
raising male children, the study revealed that although expenses for
food, housing, and medical care are higher for male children, outlays for
weddings, cosmetics, travel, jewelry, and toys are sharply higher for
female children (Olson, 1983: 40, 41, 56).

Table 2.2 divides the costs for raising children into six expenditure
categories. As you can see, the bulk of the expense that parents bear is
for food and housing. Interestingly enough, clothing—an item that
many parents feel is overpriced and that they buy often (because
children grow so much)—accounts for only 4% of the overall costs.

Of course, not all the costs of becoming a parent are financial; there
are psychological and social costs as well. Also, we should not overlook
the benefits that, in many if not most parents' minds, "make it all worth
it." When two researchers asked parents, "How is a man or woman's
life changed by having children?" the fathers and mothers in their
sample said that being a parent tied them down, resulted in a loss of
their individuality, and restricted their careers. But on the plus side,
they said that being a parent was extremely fulfilling, helped them to
grow up, made them better people, made them feel useful, gave them a

sense of achievement, and brought them a lot of happiness (Hoffman and Manis, 1978).

In sum, your future is determined, if only in part, by whether or not you have children, and it is for this reason that the decision to become a parent is perhaps the biggest decision you will ever make.

Making the Decision

The National Alliance for Optional Parenthood (NAOP), an organization founded in the 1970s to promote responsible parental decision making, publishes a pamphlet that lists a series of questions designed to help people make the right choice (Baker, 1977). Some of the questions that NAOP recommends you ask yourself *before* you go ahead and have a child are listed below.

- What do I want out of life for myself? What do I think is important?
- How would a child interfere with my growth and development?
- Do I like doing things with children? Do I enjoy activities that children can do?
- Do I want a boy or a girl child? What if I don't get what I want?
- Would I try to pass on to my child my ideas and values? What if my child's ideas and values turn out to be different from mine?
- Does my partner want to have a child? Have we talked about our reasons? Suppose one of us wants a child and the other doesn't? Who decides?

The last question is one of the most important. Becoming a parent changes you. It changes not only how you think and feel about yourself but also how you think and feel about your spouse, your friends, your parents, your job, and your religion. It even changes your sense of time and space; you never seem to have enough of either when there are kids around. The decision to become a parent thus should not be made lightly. A husband and wife should make every effort to ensure that they are in accord prior to taking on the responsibilities of parenthood—or else they may find themselves in deep trouble later on.[2]

By the way, the question of how parenthood affects marriage is one that is linked closely to historical and cultural circumstances. Only a society that separates parenthood from marriage would consider the issue worthy of investigation in the first place.

In many societies—particularly those of the historical past and of the non-Western world today—blood bonds are stronger than marital bonds, and hence the parent-child relationship is considered more important than the husband-wife relationship. Not so in the contemporary Western family system, however, and particularly "not so" within the United States today. Here, the consanguine or extended family, which cuts across several generations, has given ground to the nuclear family of husband, wife, and immediate children; kinship ties have been greatly weakened, and *children have come to be regarded almost as an appendage to, rather than a reason for, the marriage.* In other times and places, asking how parenthood affects the marriage would likely be considered inappropriate. Here and now the question is quite relevant [Christensen, 1968: 284; italics added].

You may have gotten the impression from what I have said up to now that deciding to become a parent is a simple exercise of tallying the pros and cons and then acting on the basis of which comes out on top. Nothing could be farther from the truth.

Decision making is exactly what the phrase implies: It is the act of "making" (that is, creating, constructing, or producing) a "decision" (that is, a resolution, verdict, or judgment). And it is difficult enough to do when only one person is involved; when two or more people are implicated, it can be extremely complex.

Two factors contribute to the complexity of joint decisions— *communication* and *power* (Beckman, 1982). Communication (both verbal and nonverbal) allows people to convey their thoughts, feelings, and actions to others. Communication, as was noted in Chapter 1, also is central to the social construction of values, beliefs, and norms. Hence, communication operates both as a conduit and a scaffold in the fertility decision-making process.

Power is the ability to control others. Whoever has more power in a marriage is possibly in a position to control how his or her spouse thinks and feels about parenthood and maybe even control how his or her spouse acts toward parenthood. A man, for example, who wants a child but who is married to someone who does not, could—if he has more power—change his wife's mind and convince her to stop using contraceptives.

Consider the case of Ginny and Rick. Ginny wanted to go to law school. Rick wanted her to stay home and have a child. Rick felt that Ginny's interest in pursuing a career was "inconsistent with marriage and raising children" (Sheehy, 1974: 157). Ultimately Rick won; they had their child. Here is their recollection of how they made their decision:

Ginny: Well, I specifically remember how the baby was conceived. Do you?

Rick: You refused to make love to me earlier in the evening.

Ginny: Right. And the way it finally happened added to my feeling that this was coercion. Rick had a subconscious interest in creating the situation. But Rick doesn't believe in psychological motivation.

Rick: The motivation there was very simple. I was . . .

Ginny: Interested in making love at the time! Not for the entire month, but at that particular time of the month. We didn't stop so I could put in the diaphragm, which was rare. And I got pregnant. One shot.

Rick: Very true.

Ginny: Very potent. Right? Do you remember the discussion after I got pregnant? I all but accused you of doing it so we wouldn't have to face my going to law school.

Rick: Wouldn't surprise me.

Ginny: You don't remember sitting on the couch? You had me in your arms, and I was crying.

Rick: Vaguely. All I remember is going out for dinner afterward to celebrate.

Ginny: Unbelievable! I don't remember the celebration dinner at all. [An uncomfortable silence] . . . You could interpret this argument between us as: Without Rick's sanction it would be impossible for me to go out and have a career, therefore, he has co-opted the authority to make that decision.

Rick: You cooperated. You decided you wanted to have a baby [Sheehy, 1974: 160-162].

Ginny and Rick demonstrate how complex the fertility decision-making process is. Did Ginny and Rick decide to have a baby, or did Rick make the decision for Ginny? Why would Ginny do what she claims she did not want to do? And what can we infer from the above dialogue about Ginny and Rick's ability to communicate clearly to one another? What can we infer about each's ability to attach meanings to situations?

Answers are difficult to come by, but we can say this much. Other sections of this case (not reproduced here) strongly suggest that Rick has more power in the marriage than Ginny. Thus, it is entirely possible that Ginny is right when she says that she felt "coerced" into having a baby. However, Rick did not rape Ginny, so to some extent Rick is correct when he says that she "cooperated." But to say that she "decided" she wanted to have a baby, as he does at the end, is misleading and a good illustration of how people construct definitions of situations. If eventually Rick can convince Ginny that she chose to have a baby, the fallout from their act will be minimized. If not, the conflict could destroy their marriage. As to the discrepancy between their memories of what happened when Ginny learned that she was pregnant, this is but one example of how different these two people are. Come to think of it, the fact that they are so different may be the source of their problems. Not only can they not convey to each other how they think and feel, they do not seem to be able to understand or value the other's point of view.

One final note on how husbands and wives make the decision to become parents. It is estimated that 40% of all pregnancies are mistimed and that 15% are unwanted. Most of these mistimed and unwanted pregnancies are the result of no contraception being used at all or of failed or discontinued contraception. Approximately 41% of these mistimed or unwanted pregnancies end with a child being born; the rest are terminated by abortion or miscarriage. This 41% translates into about 1,373,000 babies born each year in the United States who are unintended (Ory et al., 1983: 15), which means that there are a lot of children in this country who, in some respects, are uninvited guests in their own homes.

Childless by Choice

Some couples consciously decide *not* to become parents. About 5.5 million ever-married women aged 15 to 44 are childless, and 683,000 of these (or about 2%) are childless by choice. The rest are either involuntarily childless or are delaying having children (Mosher and Bachrach, 1982).

Studies indicate that there are basically two kinds of voluntarily childless people: rejectors and aficionados.

Rejectors are primarily motivated by *reaction* against the *di*sadvantages of having children. . . . Rejectors often tend to dislike children, and to avoid being around them. A number of them flaunt their childlessness; others actively proselytize their antinatalist ideology and childfree lifestyle. Aficionados are persons who are ardent devotees of voluntary childlessness because they appreciate the *advantages* of being childfree, rather than the disadvantages of parenthood. . . . Generally, they like children, or at least have a neutral attitude towards them, and on the issue of natalism, they tend to be apolitical, endorsing neither the pronatalist nor the antinatalist perspective [Veevers, 1980: 158].

These same studies also reveal that enroute to a child-free lifestyle, most couples pass through four separate stages.

(1) *Postponement for a definite time:* Husband and wife defer childbearing to graduate from school, buy a house, or simply get adjusted to one another.
(2) *Postponement for an indefinite time:* Husband and wife remain committed to becoming parents, but become increasingly vague as to when.
(3) *Deliberating the pros and cons of parenthood:* A qualitative change takes place, in that there is an open acknowledgment of the possibility that, in the end, they may choose not to have children.
(4) *Acceptance of permanent childlessness:* Couple comes to the conclusion that childlessness is a permanent rather than a transitory state [Veevers, 1980: 20-27].

The fact that most husbands and wives today take a long time to decide to remain childless accentuates something I said earlier. Not many decisions are as important as the decision to become, or not become, a parent. No matter which way you go, your life will be altered forever.

CONCLUSION

Fertility is not simply a biological outcome; it is also a social process. Children do not appear out of the blue; they are decided into existence. And because all decisions are made in a historical and societal context, the decision to become a parent—however personal it may seem to you—is a public issue of the highest order (Mills, 1959).

In short, who has children and why has always been and continues to be one of the most important questions that humanity confronts. The future of the world literally depends on how we deal with this social issue.

In this chapter I have tried to convey both the breadth and depth of the fertility question. I began with a discussion of fertility rates in the United States—showing how they have changed and how they vary by age and socioeconomic status—and concluded with an examination of the structure and dynamics of the fertility decision-making process. The next chapter picks up where this one ends, in that it focuses on the immediate consequences rather than causes of conception.

REVIEW QUESTIONS

(1) How did people control fertility in the past? How do they control fertility today?

(2) How has the fertility rate in the United States changed since World War II, and how does it vary today by age and socioeconomic status?

(3) What are the pros and cons of becoming a parent? What are the pros and cons of remaining childfree?

(4) If two of your friends told you that they were in the midst of making the decision to become parents and you were interested in studying the process that led to their choice, one way or the other, what factors would you focus on and why?

SUGGESTED ASSIGNMENTS

(1) Go to the library and locate recent volumes of the journal, *Family Planning Perspectives*. Read several of the articles to learn more about the issues raised in this chapter.

(2) Call one of the hospitals in your area and make an appointment to talk to members of the staff who either teach sex education or perform abortions. Try to get a sense of how they view their job.

(3) Interview a husband and wife who have chosen not to have children. Ask them to reconstruct for you how they went about making their decision.

NOTES

1. When computing a fecundity rate or fertility rate, demographers generally focus on women aged 15 to 44. Thus, strictly speaking, the *fecundity rate* is the number of children that women aged 15 to 44 are biologically able to bear, and the (general) *fertility rate* is the number of births divided by the number of women aged 15 to 44. Also, the fertility rate and the birth rate are not the same thing. The (crude) *birth rate* is the number of births divided by the size of the population. I intend to examine fertility rates rather than fecundity or birth rates because fertility rates are more relevant to understanding the process of becoming a parent.

2. This book focuses primarily on what happens to married people who become parents and does not examine the social reality of out-of-wedlock birth. I trust that a future volume in the family-text series will deal with this complex and important topic.

CHAPTER
3

Pregnancy

ASKED WHAT IT WAS LIKE to be an expectant mother, one woman remarked, "You think that it's all in your womb and then you find out that your whole life is pregnant" (Boston Women's Health Book Collective, 1978: 34). In a few words this mother-to-be has conveyed not only the essence of her pregnancy experience but the rationale behind this chapter as well. For in the pages that follow I hope to give you some idea of how people's lives—both men's and women's—are changed by the discovery that they have conceived a child and are about to become parents.

THE CONNECTION BETWEEN
THE PHYSICAL AND SOCIAL PREGNANCY

Let me begin by saying that there are at least two realities of pregnancy: the physical and the social (or, as the expectant mother phrased it, there is the change that takes place in the womb and the change that takes place in your life). The physical reality of pregnancy begins at the moment of fertilization, when a man's sperm enters a woman's ovum and the nuclei of the two fuse together to form a new cell called a zygote. If the zygote is healthy and is not subsequently aborted, it will develop inside the woman's uterus and about nine months later travel through her vagina (or through her abdomen in case of a cesarean section) to become a new baby boy or girl.[1] By contrast, the social reality of pregnancy begins not at the moment of fertilization but when someone believes that he or she is expecting a child; it begins when a person claims the right to be called an expectant father or mother (for example, "My wife and I are going to have a baby" or "I believe that I am pregnant") (Miller, 1978). The physical reality and social reality of pregnancy need not coincide. A woman, for example, may be unaware that she is carrying a baby; a man may think his wife is pregnant when she is not. Also, some individuals may be more willing than others to accept being pregnant: For instance, a husband and wife who have been trying for a long time to have a baby may be quick to interpret any physical cue (a missed period, nausea) as a sign that their wish has been granted.

One of the first studies to note the distinction (and sometimes contradiction) between the physical and the social pregnancy is sociologist Rita Seiden-Miller's study of 49 women who were expecting their first child (Miller, 1978). Miller discovered not only that the social pregnancy exists but also that it is composed of at least three stages.

The *first stage*, which generally occurs during the first two months of the physical pregnancy, begins when someone (women in her study) begins to interpret various bodily changes as omens of pregnancy and begins to see herself as an expectant parent. Wondering whether people who planned to have a baby would pass through this stage more quickly than those who did not, Miller divided her sample into three groups—the true planners, the sort-of planners, and the nonplanners—and analyzed the degree to which the women in each group relied on other people to interpret whether they were pregnant. As you might expect, the true planners were more likely to say that they diagnosed their own condition, whereas the sort-of planners and nonplanners typically relied on others to interpret the signs. Miller notes that "the non-planners relied almost exclusively on 'official' [physicians'] inter-pretations of physical cues," and many reported "not even having a hunch" that they were pregnant until they were told so by someone who was medically trained (Miller, 1978: 191-192).

The heavy reliance of nonplanners on a medical diagnosis may not be as true today as it was when Miller conducted her study. Nowadays, women can determine whether they are pregnant by using a com-mercial pregnancy test available at most drugstores.

Even though a man or woman may know that he or she is going to have a baby, it apparently is still hard to believe, especially if it is early, before the woman can feel the baby's movement, and before her body has begun to noticeably change. A number of women in Miller's sample initially had only a tentative attachment to their new identities, remarking that it did not "seem very real" because they did not "feel different" or "look different." However, when noticeable changes began to take place, between the second through sixth months, the women entered the *second stage* of the social pregnancy, the stage during which, in their minds, they became "definitely" pregnant. For many women the critical change was *quickening*—the point at which fetal motion is felt.

When I first felt the baby move, it was really like the first step, you know, that it was really something happening. Until then it was just something we talked about [Miller, 1978: 196].

The transformation from a tentative to a definite pregnancy identity was facilitated not only by the physical changes but also by the social interactions generated by these changes. Visiting the doctor regularly, donning maternity clothes (a costume that heightened both their own and other people's sense of their new identity), and talking day in and day out about being an expectant mother all helped to make the pregnancy "real" to the women.

The *third stage* of the social pregnancy (months six to nine) is characterized by a preoccupation with labor and delivery and with life as a parent—what one author (Whelan, 1978) has called "infantici-pating." Although expectant fathers and mothers will think about birth and parenthood well before the end of the pregnancy, these issues understandably become especially salient as the due date draws near. As one woman who was in her ninth month realized,

We were visiting with friends last week and their kids really got on my nerves. I was so thankful to get back to the peace and quiet of our apartment. Then I thought, "Oh, my God, that's what this place will be like soon!" [Whelan, 1978: 131].

It is also during the final months that expectant parents typically will settle on a name, buy clothes for the baby, and arrange for day care if needed.

EXPECTANT MOTHERS

There is a strongly held belief in America and virtually everywhere else that having children is a woman's destiny and the source of her identity. Becoming a mother thus is perceived as a significant transition—perhaps *the* most significant transition—in a woman's life (Rossi, 1968). At the same time, motherhood generally is not viewed as a prestigious occupation in this society, and consequently it is not uncommon to find women who, when asked what they "do," are embarrassed to say that mothering is their "job" (LaRossa and LaRossa, 1981).

The fact that motherhood is depicted as both important and menial is one reason that many women have ambivalent feelings about being pregnant. Even women whose pregnancies were planned often will find themselves having both positive and negative attitudes toward parenthood (Lederman, 1984).

According to one study (Hanford, 1968), these conflicting feelings are very strong at the beginning of the pregnancy but taper off as the birth date draws near. The explanation offered is that, as the pregnancy progresses, the expectant mother will engage in a series of behaviors designed to reduce her ambivalence. For example, she will try to remember the positive aspects of having children and forget the negative, often by seeking out people who will accentuate the good things about parenthood—her own mother may be helpful in this regard—and avoiding others who might remind her of the drawbacks—for example, her voluntarily childless friends.

Interestingly enough, a more recent study (Leifer, 1980) found just the opposite—that instead of there being a decline in the level of conflict from one week to the next, women viewed their pregnancies with *increased* ambivalence as time went on.

Why the difference of opinion between the two studies? Apart from the fact that each study used different measures of conflict, the disparity also may reflect the changes that have taken place in this country during the time that the two studies were completed (1968 versus 1980). The reduction in conflict to which the first study alludes hinges on the success of the various ambivalence-reducing strategies; if these strategies are ineffective, intrapsychic conflict presumably would remain constant or increase. The second study says that women become more ambivalent toward pregnancy because the physical and social limitations during the latter stages of the pregnancy (for example, fatigue and changes in marriage) prove to be more extreme than they anticipated. Thus, the key to both studies appears to be the discrepancy between expectations and perceived realities (see Oakley, 1980: 281). It just might be that women today are less willing to accept the constraints that pregnancy imposes, in part because they are less likely to find others who are willing to define these constraints in positive terms. If this is the case, then we would not be surprised to discover that pregnancy is a more difficult *social* experience for women today than, say, 20 years ago; and we would hypothesize that women who are highly committed to nonparental activities (their jobs or marriages) would have the most difficult time adjusting to pregnancy (see, for example, Behrman, 1982; Lederman, 1984).

Mothers-to-be actually must learn to deal with a host of contradictory expectations (Graham, 1976). On the one hand, "the pregnant woman is seen as strong and powerful because of her demonstrated fertility and fulfilled identity," but she is also "viewed as vulnerable and frail" (Leifer, 1980: 19). With respect to the perception of vulnerability and frailty, many women undoubtedly like to be viewed as helpless when they are pregnant and to be catered to as a result. Some even relish the idea. As one woman whom I interviewed said, "I love being pregnant. I've never gotten so much attention in my life." Another reported, "I just have a feeling that I can say anything I feel like saying and nobody dares do anything about it!" (LaRossa, 1977: 48, 146). Most women, however, seem to object to being considered "sick" when they are pregnant (Entwisle and Doering, 1981: 54) because it almost invariably means that they are thrust into a "child-like, dependent role" (Breen, 1975: 54). Mothers-to-be whose sex-role orientation is distinctly modern, perhaps feminist, are especially uneasy with the idea that they are sick when they are pregnant (Gladieux, 1978).

The belief that pregnancy is a "delicate condition" is not new by any means. Throughout history mothers-to-be have had to contend with a number of superstitions and folk remedies that, if ignored, presumably spelled trouble for them and their babies. During the eighteenth century, for example, pregnant women were told

- not to live in dirty narrow lanes or near common dunghills, lest the bad smells cause miscarriage,
- to avoid loud noises (specifically, thunder, artillery, and great bells) and to abstain from riding on horseback or in coaches or wagons for the same reason,
- not to exercise because doing so will turn a fetus sideways or in some other wrong posture,

- not to sleep after dinner, for lives of "idle luxury" resulted in sickly children,
- never to bathe in hot water, lest the womb open,
- to wear an ingot of steel between their breasts to keep the breasts from growing too big and to stop their milk from curdling,
- not to eat fish, lentils, beans, fried food, milk, fruit, cheese, salads, spiced meats, or too much salt meat (the last "would make the child be born without nails, a sign of short life"), and
- to subject themselves to periodic bleeding to purge themselves of their "bad blood" [Eccles, 1982: 62-64].

And today? Well, ideas about health and nutrition have definitely changed. Pregnant women are now told

- to continue to work outside the home until the onset of labor, provided the job is not any more hazardous than daily life,
- to do a moderate amount of exercising,
- to rest frequently and take naps whenever possible,
- to avoid starches and pastries and to eat protein-rich and energy-rich foods (for example, lean meat, fish, chicken, cottage cheese, salads, vegetables, fruits),
- to abstain from smoking and drinking alcoholic beverages,
- to steer clear of a variety of chemicals, including lead, mercury, vinyl chloride, carbon monoxide, and any and all pesticides, and
- to take a daily shower or bath, but to avoid soaking in a hot tub (102° F or higher) for more than a few minutes [Birch, 1982].

Medical policy on prenatal (prebirth) care actually has changed a lot over the past 20 years. Today, doctors tell us that whatever an expectant mother eats or drinks or whatever is injected into her bloodstream may eventually make its way to the baby growing inside her. But up until the 1960s doctors did not believe this to be the case. The popular medical view then was that the fetus was insulated from the mother. Drugs given to the mother, for example, generally were not seen as potential threats to the fetus. What made doctors change their minds was the thalidomide tragedy.

In 1961-62 an unprecedented outbreak of phocomolia, a congenital malformation characterized by severe defects of the long bones, resulting in what is commonly known as "flippers," missing limbs, was observed in Western Europe primarily, and throughout Europe and the United States to a lesser extent. At least 5,000 infants were involved. It was later documented that the defects were related to the use of a tranquilizing drug, thalidomide, during the thirtieth to fiftieth day of pregnancy. In many cases the thalidomide was taken on prescription from obstetricians for the control of nausea during pregnancy. That thousands of infants were dramatically damaged by a substance ingested by their mothers directly contradicted the medical model, which believed the fetus to be insulated and protected within the womb. The placenta, as a result of this experience, was no longer seen as as a shield or barrier for the infant; instead it came to be seen as a "bloody sieve" [Rothman, 1982: 135-136].

The thalidomide tragedy and, more recently, the DES tragedy (whereby it was discovered that a synthetic hormone, diethylistilbestrol or DES, given to women in the 1940s and 1950s to guard against miscarriage, could cause cancer in their daughters 15 to 40 years later) not only forced the medical profession to modify its obstetrical models but also prompted people to question seriously the validity of obstetrical practice. For the first time since the nineteenth century, when doctors fought midwives for the control of pregnancy and birth (to be discussed in Chapter 4), obstetricians find themselves under considerable scrutiny and have been placed on the defensive. It is now common for couples to interview obstetricians to decide which one is best for them; and doctors are learning that their word is not always law, that more and more women expect to take an active part in whatever decisions are to be made about their own case. In short, the "you don't need to know, just sit and grow" medical position (Rorvick and Shettles, 1970: 31) no longer is considered acceptable (McBride, 1982: 420).

All of this is probably good, given the condescending attitude toward women that had developed over the years in the field of obstetrics. Here, for example, is an excerpt from a book entitled *Confessions of a Gynecologist*, published in 1972, that reflects to some degree the kind of arrogance of which many obstetricians were guilty at the time.

Thirty years spent largely in dealing with pregnant women ought to entitle any man to some sort of medal, say one showing a stork, rampant, holding a telephone in one foot and a speculum in the other. I don't intend to claim mine, however, until I have found the solution for one problem which, more than any other, gets parturient females into trouble and threatens to turn me into a mean old man. That problem is a three letter word: F-A-T.

A day in my office can be going happily, smoothly, with no complications. Then the nurse tells me that Mrs. B, a thoroughly nice patient and well along in her pregnancy, has weighed in at 154 pounds, up seven since her last visit. My spirits plummet. I delay, smoke a cigarette before going into the examining room, to cool off. Mrs. B needs that extra seven pounds like she needs two heads. In fact, an extra head with a bit more willpower might help her. . . .

As I come in, I glance at her ankles. If they are swollen, indicating edema—water in the tissues—the gain may not be her fault and the problem can be treated with diuretics. But if her ankles are nice and trim and the flab in her belly was put there by potatoes, butter, pies, cake, and ice cream, she is going to get a lecture [Anonymous M.D., 1972: 55-56].

There are two things about Dr. Anonymous's comments that are worth noting. First, there is his patronizing attitude. His demeanor suggests a strong desire to control his patients, to be the boss. (Elsewhere, he admits that he is disappointed that his patients no longer regard him "as a sort of demi-God who can do no wrong.") We can probably assume that his definition of a good patient is one who blindly follows his orders, and no doubt he believes that this approach is in the best interest of the mothers. Interestingly enough, however, studies indicate that women who adopt a passive role during pregnancy—who allow themselves to be controlled by their doctors, families, and friends—are more likely to suffer both pre- and postpartum depression (Breen, 1975). Also, women who regard pregnancy as a debilitating illness typically experience more medical complications (Rosengren, 1962). It is thus both psychologically and medically beneficial that there are fewer obstetricians like Dr. Anonymous around (and that those who are like him have been put on notice by their patients to change).

The second thing worth noting about the doctor's comments is his philosophy about weight gain during pregnancy. The reason he is monitoring his patient's weight is that he is concerned about edema and, ultimately, toxemia, a blood disease unique to human pregnancy. At the time he wrote his book most obstetricians felt pretty much the same way as he did, namely that excessive weight gain led to toxemia. Today, however, doctors realize that this is not the case. Too much weight gain may result in operative complications, but toxemia is not one of them.

Of course, doctors are not the only ones concerned about weight gain; mothers are concerned too, but typically for different reasons. Given the emphasis that our society places on being thin, it is not unusual to find women who feel ugly when they are pregnant because they associate being pregnant with being "fat." During interviews that I conducted with expectant couples several years ago, how the wife looked was very much a topic of concern, and in almost every case *how the husband felt about how the wife looked* was especially important. Unfortunately for the women in my study, the husbands were not particulary complimentary.

> Fitz: I'm just getting sick of seeing you fat!
> Fran: Me too!
>
>   * * *
>
> Interviewer: Do you find Nancy just as desirable [as you did before the pregnancy]?
> Norman: Well, I don't know. She looks pretty good in clothes, and in the dark you can't see so it's not so bad.
> Interviewer: How do you feel about that, Nancy?
> Norman: She knows it's true.
> Nancy: I know [LaRossa, 1977: 142].

Needless to say, even if a mother-to-be is treated as a normal human being by her husband (and family and friends), she is not necessarily immune to ridicule, for she must still contend with the reaction of strangers. One woman noted,

> People stare, unbelievably. Pregnant women must be [the] most awkward-looking things to other people, and I never realized, but I can walk down the street and people will just stare. . . . I think to myself, My God, I must be a freak. And it's a little amusing, but it also angers me, it's like when you're a teenager and men whistle at you, a very humiliating feeling somehow [Leifer, 1980: 25].

In one study, strangers not only stared at an apparently pregnant woman, they also went out of their way not to stand close to her (Taylor and Langer, 1977). Men were also more likely than women to exhibit avoidance behavior. For example, several men who entered an elevator and who at first were oblivious to the woman's "condition" visibly backed off and moved quickly to the elevator's far side upon discovering that she was pregnant. These findings indicate that, although expectant mothers have more freedom than they once had—it is no longer considered in poor taste for them to appear in public or be featured on a TV show (see Sorel, 1984:83; Wertz and Wertz, 1977: 79-80)—they still

are viewed as oddities. In other words, mothers-to-be are treated much
the same as people with obvious physical disabilities: "They are stared
at, avoided, and generally treated as less human by the 'normal' people
around them" (Taylor and Langer, 1977: 27).

EXPECTANT FATHERS

After discovering that they are about to become fathers, many men
are content to allow the spotlight to shine on their wives, while they stay
in the background, watching and waiting. The few men who want to
share the glory and excitement often are shunted aside. (I know one
expectant couple whose friends offered to host a baby shower,
provided that the husband, who had expressed a genuine interest in
participating, not be invited. The couple was told that baby showers are
"for women only.")
All of this may seem "natural," given that it is the woman and not the
man who is carrying the baby. But this attitude overlooks the fact that,
although the wife is the only one physically pregnant, both the husband
and the wife are socially pregnant. Sociologists also are guilty of
overlooking fathers-to-be. In contrast to the vast number of studies of
expectant mothers, there is only a handful of studies of expectant
fathers.
The differences between expectant motherhood and expectant
fatherhood are pretty much what you would think. Expectant mothers
look unique; expectant fathers do not. Thus, expectant fathers are not
stared at or avoided as expectant mothers are. The physical reality of
pregnancy also means that expectant fathers do not have anywhere
near the amount of medical contact during pregnancy that expectant
mothers have.
What about the similarities between expectant motherhood and
expectant fatherhood? If we focus on the social side of pregnancy, we
discover that there are a number of parallels.
Perhaps the most important similarity is that, as is the case with
women, men who are committed to their careers are more likely to view
pregnancy as an intrusion and are more likely to postpone or avoid
accepting the responsibilities associated with impending parenthood
(McCorkel, 1964). One business executive, upon being told by his wife
that she was pregnant, was so stunned at the prospect of being a father
that, without saying anything, he turned around and went straight to his

den. The wife retreated to the bedroom to cry. After about an hour, the husband came out, half-heartedly put his arms around his wife, and said simply, "It will work out okay" (Whelan, 1978: 52-54). Apparently, career-oriented men and women, although still interested in having children, are anxious about the potential conflicts between their parental and occupational roles.

Second, men, like women, feel pride upon discovering that they are about to have a child, which is perfectly understandable. It is pleasing to know that you can conceive a baby—that your reproductive organs do work and that you are on the brink of becoming a link in the great chain of humanity. Vanity also may have something to do with it. Knowing that you are about to replicate yourself, that there will be another *you* to admire, is an intoxicating idea.

Women are likely to see their ability to bear children as something that makes them strong and powerful. So, too, men are prone to view their ability to procreate as a sign of their vigor and authority. I once interviewed a man who said that seeing his wife pregnant made him "feel kind of like King Kong" (LaRossa, 1977: 144).

Because women are the ones who carry the fetus during pregnancy, it is not unusual for them to assume that the fetus is more theirs than their husbands'. But men too have been known to make similar property claims. In ancient times people believed that within each sperm there dwelled a miniature person (called a homunculus) waiting to grow inside a woman's uterus. In other words, the expectant mother was perceived as little more than an incubator for the man's child (Eccles, 1982: 37). About ten years ago, singer and composer Paul Anka was criticized for implying a similarly male chauvinistic view of pregnancy when he recorded a song entitled "You're Having My Baby." Many women felt that the song's title and lyrics were offensive because they suggested that children belong to men.

Finally, like their wives, expectant fathers often are depicted as incompetent children.

> Classically, the will-be-father is pictured putting on his clothes backward—that is, if he puts them on at all—as he rushes off to the hospital; being unable to get the car started and getting lost on the way; when he finally arrives, calling for a wheelchair and getting into it himself [Whelan, 1978: 156-157].

Funny as this may be, the denigration of expectant fathers has been instrumental in keeping them on the periphery of the social pregnancy experience and, in some cases, has deprived them of the opportunity to support their wives just when their wives needed them most (Kitzinger, 1978: 77).

PREGNANCY AND MARRIAGE

What effect does pregnancy have on the husband-wife relationship? This is a question that is being asked more and more nowadays, first, because of the premium that people today place on having emotionally satisfying marriages (thus, anything that might alter an otherwise good marriage is subject to scrutiny); and, second, because of the theoretical interest in families as systems (thus, marriages are conceptualized as systems that can change during pregnancy).

Sexual Relations

For most couples, pregnancy reduces both sexual desire and the frequency of intercourse. The last trimester generally is when sexual appetite and activity are at their lowest (Calhoun et al., 1981).

It is hard to say why pregnancy results in a decline in marital sex. In a study that I conducted, expectant couples gave 19 differenent excuses or justifications to explain why their sex life had changed (LaRossa, 1979). When people offer *excuses* for their behavior, they basically are saying that what is happening is bad but that it is not their fault. When they offer *justifications*, they accept responsibility for what is happening, but claim that the situation is not as bad as it appears (Scott and Lyman, 1968). The couples' excuses placed the blame either on something (Type I excuse) or on someone (Type II excuse), and their justifications cited either self-fulfillment (Type I justification) or priorities (Type II justification). Table 3.1 provides a breakdown of the excuses and justifications offered by 12 of the 16 couples in the sample.

Because there were so few couples in the study, the distribution of excuses and justifications in Table 3.1 cannot be considered representative of any specified population. The rationale behind the study, however, was not to survey the sexual attitudes of parents-to-be, but to propose hypotheses for future research. You see, most studies of sex during pregnancy focus primarily on changes in sexual desire or behavior and give little or no attention to the reasons for these changes.

TABLE 3.1
Frequency of Reasons for Changes in Sex During Pregnancy

Type of Reason	Husbands (N = 12)*	Wives
Type I Excuses: Physiological/Anatomical		
wife too tired	2	1
wife sick (nausea, vomiting)	2	
wife's sex drive decreased		2
mentally want more, physically want less		1
wife's body too big and clumsy		2
wife's hormonal change		1
Type II Excuses: Biographical/Sociocultural		
wife not attractive or sexy	3	6
sex now sacrilegious	1	1
sex is for procreation	1	1
motherhood and sex conflict	2	
baby's presence felt		1
book said stop		1
doctor said stop		1
"hangups" from parents or society		1
husband unaware of wife's feelings		1
Type I Justifications: Self-Fulfillment		
couple feels close, sex unnecessary	2	1
energies channeled toward baby	2	
Type II Justifications: Priorities		
fear of hurting baby	3	6
fear of hurting wife	3	2

SOURCE: Ralph LaRossa (1979) "Sex during pregnancy: A symbolic interactionist analysis." Journal of Sex Research 15 (May): 119-128. Reprinted with permission from the Society for the Scientific Study of Sex.
*Columns total more than 12 because subjects volunteered more than one reason. The number of reasons offered ranged from 1 to 10 (mean = 4.6).

But if we are interested in understanding the social reality of pregnancy, we cannot afford to relegate these reasons to a subordinate status, for the reasons that expectant parents offer for changes in their sexual interests and behavior are part and parcel of the social reality of pregnancy itself.

Theoretically speaking, these excuses and justifications are *aligning actions*, by which I mean they are rhetorical strategies designed to bridge a gap between norms and behavior (Stokes and Hewitt, 1976). Thus, when people offer excuses or justifications they tacitly are acknowledging that a breach of conduct has taken place and are hoping that their explanation will be sufficient to mend the gap. This is brought home by the fact that in my study I never asked the couples *why* their sex lives had changed; I asked them only *if* there was a change. In other words, most of the couples said that there was a decline in interest and in intercourse and then, *on their own initiative*, went on to offer excuses and justifications for the decline. Indirectly, the couples were communicating that, in their minds, a decline in marital sex conflicted with the norms of marriage, in which sex is not simply permitted but required (Broderick, 1975), and they were hoping that I would honor their excuses and justifications and not think of them as "weird" or "abnormal."

The practical relevance of understanding the role that sexual aligning actions play during pregnancy is illustrated by the husband and wife who had the most difficulty coping with changes in their sexual activity. As soon as the wife discovered that she was pregnant, she began to reject her husband's advances without telling him why (that is, without offering an excuse or justification). In the absence of an explanation from his wife, the husband (who, as a truck driver, was often away from home for a good part of the day) began to come up with explanations of his own—and some of the conclusions he started to draw were making him angry.

> Fran: It must have looked like I was going out on the town, you know?
> Fitz: That did cross my mind! You go to work for eight hours, and you're over there thinking "There's somebody with her," and this does go through a guy's mind. I'm up north driving trucks and some nights I'd leave for work at four in the morning, and I wouldn't get home until eight at night. And here I am, driving a truck, just thinking of who's here. It does go through your mind. And you come home, and you go to give her a kiss and she turns her head. Jesus, it seems like you're just coming home to sleep. It was that way for two or three weeks. . . . Then you have the thought coming to your mind: "Is that my baby?" Really. I had some weird thoughts over those three weeks [LaRossa, 1978: 9].

As Fitz notes, the crisis lasted only about three weeks. What seems to have broken the logjam, however, was Fran's fear that Fitz would *rape* her. Hoping to ward him off, she excused her behavior by saying that her sex drive had decreased and justified her behavior by claiming that she was afraid that she would hurt the baby. Fitz was appeased. As long as he believed he knew why his wife was shunning him, he could accept not making love to her for the duration of the pregnancy.

By the way, current medical wisdom is that sexual relations during a healthy pregnancy are not harmful to either the mother or fetus. Couples may have to be creative, as some of their favorite positions may prove uncomfortable. But rarely are expectant couples told to abstain from sex altogether (Birch, 1982). All of which means that, from a medical point of view, several of the reasons listed in Table 3.1 are fallacious. What is important, however, from a sociological point of view, is whether expectant couples *believe* their own motivations. For in the social world, if people define situations as real, they are real in their consequences (W. I. Thomas, cited in Blumer, 1939).

Emotional Closeness

You might think that with the decline in their sexual activity, expectant fathers and mothers would complain that the quality of their marriages had also deteriorated. The fact is, however, that most expectant fathers and mothers report that pregnancy has made their marriages better—that they feel closer, more connected (Lederman, 1984; McCorkel, 1964; Shereshefsky and Yarrow, 1973).

Of course, some couples simply may be reporting what they wish were true. Finding their sex lives temporarily stalled, they may pretend that their marriages have improved and conclude that everything is not so bad after all. The three people in my study who said that the decline in their sexual activity was not a problem because of how close their marriages had become may fall into this category. To argue, however, that most couples are lying or kidding themselves when they report increased feelings of intimacy is wrong because there are a number of things about pregnancy that, indeed, can have an impact on the quality of marital life.

First of all, pregnancy provides couples with a common focus. Plans need to be made, baby items must be purchased, names have to be chosen. Each of these responsibilities provides opportunities for husbands and wives to be together and to share ideas, hopes, and fears.

Second, husbands tend to be more solicitous to their pregnant wives. That is, they tend to go out of their way to be nice and more understanding. The "solicitous expectant father role" is not a recent invention; on the contrary, it has been around for quite some time. During the seventeenth century,

> A pregnant woman's mood was deemed crucial to her own welfare and that of the child-to-be. Accordingly her husband was enjoined to demonstrate sympathy by using kind words and providing her with whatever she wanted [Fox and Quitt, 1980: 35].

Finally, many couples see the fetus as a concrete representation of their love. For some, simply thinking about the baby is enough to strengthen the marital bond.

Although most husbands and wives feel more connected during pregnancy, not everyone's marriage improves at the same rate. Generally speaking, the more family-oriented a person is, the more intimate his or her marriage becomes (Goshen-Gottstein, 1966; McCorkel, 1964). Also, the more egalitarian a couple's marriage is, the closer and more integrated the marriage becomes (Grossman et al., 1980).

The Division of Labor in the Home

Research indicates that the household division of labor (that is, who prepares the meals, does the dishes, mows the lawn) is not affected appreciably by the onset of pregnancy. Some expectant fathers have been found to do more around the house than before, and some expectant mothers have been found to do less. But the data available show that expectant couples do not significantly alter the way they allocate housework (Entwisle and Doering, 1981: 35; Oakley, 1980: 132).

It is surprising that husbands and wives do not change in this regard. You would think that because pregnant women often are cast in a sick role, they would be absolved of many household responsibilities. One explanation is that mothers-to-be *do* perform fewer duties around the house but not at their husband's expense; the house may be allowed to get dirtier and more meals may be eaten out. Another possibility is that, although there are exceptions, most expectant mothers *want* to continue to cook and clean as much as before because to do otherwise is to accept the sick role, which they would just as soon not do. And still a third possibility is that husbands may be *reluctant* to change, that they prefer that their wives—pregnant or not—continue to do most of the housework, and they communicate this preference when they find themselves doing more than they deem necessary or desirable. The following is a case in point.

Like many husbands of pregnant wives, Daryl expected that every now and then he would be expected to do more around the house. What he evidently did not anticipate or like was Debby's attempts to normalize his helping her. By *normalize* I mean redefining an activity from atypical (and therefore worthy of recognition) to typical. For instance, before she was pregnant Debby would carry the dirty clothes up the hill to the car for transportation to the laundromat ("up the hill" because their house was situated in a small ravine). Thus, for her to request that Daryl do it was atypical and worthy of recognition ("Thank you for doing something that you don't normally have to do"). But when she became pregnant, and especially toward the end when she was getting quite large, it seems that Debby began to take it for granted that Daryl would carry the laundry to the car, thereby normalizing his assistance. Daryl sensed and apparently resented the change in the status quo, and asked Debby for an explanation. (Note, again, the importance of aligning actions.)

> Debby: It [the laundry] is just too heavy.
> Daryl: Oh. I see.
> Debby: It gets very awkward trying to carry that laundry basket when you're carrying it out far. You don't have quite the sense of balance that you do when it's close to you.
> Daryl: Yes, but you *could* do it.
> Debby: Yea, I could do it.
> Daryl: Well, why didn't you do it?
> Debby: Why not let *you* do it?
> Daryl: I don't know. I'm just trying to figure out why you didn't do it.
> Debby: I just didn't feel like it. Besides, it was an excuse not to go to the laundromat anymore.
> Interviewer: So you've been doing the laundry more, Daryl?
> Daryl: No, I haven't been doing it, but coming up this hill several months previously, she would carry it up the hill. Now there's no question that I carry it up the hill [LaRossa, 1977: 46-47].

Daryl and Debby's conversation suggests yet another reason that studies have not uncovered significant changes in the division of household labor during pregnancy. Studies of the division of the labor in families almost always focus on major household tasks, such as doing the laundry, but ignore related tasks, such as carrying the laundry to the car. In Daryl and Debby's marriage, who does the laundry has not changed but who carries the laundry to the car has. Thus, how they divide the housework *has changed*, but not in a way that is likely to be noticed in a standard survey. Researchers may be failing to pick up changes in the division of household labor during pregnancy because they are using measures that are insensitive to minor variations in who does what.

Marital Power

The balance of power in any relationship, marital or otherwise, is a function of two interrelated factors: ideology and dependence (Scanzoni, 1979). *Ideology* refers to the beliefs about power to which people subscribe. If, for example, a couple believes that the husband should be in charge because their religion dictates that the man should be the head of the house, then there is a good chance that the husband will have more power in the marriage. *Dependence* refers to how reliant people are on one another. Generally speaking, power is inversely related to dependency. The more dependent you are on someone, the less power you have vis-à-vis that person. Thus, if a wife is dependent on her husband not only for economic support but for socioemotional support as well (for example, she desperately needs his affection and love), then there is, once again, a good chance that the husband will have more power in the marriage.

During pregnancy a number of events can take place to alter the balance of marital power. A couple might believe that a pregnant woman is under duress, incapable of thinking clearly, and in need of someone (for example, her husband) to guide her. If so, the power in this marriage might shift more toward the husband. Or a woman might quit her job toward the end of the pregnancy with the intention of becoming a full-time homemaker and mother. If this means that she now will be financially dependent on her husband, then she may lose some power vis-à-vis her spouse. One expectant father, for example, whose wife was about to give up her job, felt that he would be gaining power as a result:

> Now she's going to be the housewife and I'm going to be the principal breadwinner. That moves me up a notch in terms of being the bread-

winner and having the say in financial matters. . . . Because I will be the sole breadwinner, my authority will go up slightly [LaRossa, 1977: 79].

This particular husband was more sensitive than most to his wife's new role. At the end of the pregnancy, after she had stopped working, he was annoyed with the fact that she periodically received calls for assistance from her former coworkers (for example, "Where's the X file?"). In fact, he was so annoyed that he threatened to get violent.

If they call up here . . . I'm going to tell them, "Hey, you'd better hang up now, and if you call once more, I'm going to punch you in the mouth" [LaRossa, 1977: 82].

There is a possibility that the violent threat was really aimed at his wife, because he had admitted hitting her once when she supposedly had tried to "dominate" him ("I got angry and slapped her in the face three or four times"). I mention the violence because studies indicate that women are more likely to be abused by their husbands during pregnancy (Gelles, 1975; Giles-Sims, 1983). Because violence and power are interrelated—violence often is used as a way of maintaining or gaining power when other strategies fail (Goode, 1971)—the discovery that women are "at risk" when they are pregnant suggests that struggles for power may be very common during pregnancy. One can only hope that in the future—as women grow less dependent on their husbands and as men come to realize that women are not for hitting—struggles for power during pregnancy will become rare, and violence toward mothers-to-be (and women in general) will become nonexistent.

CONCLUSION

Becoming a parent means having to traverse a social as well as a physical pregnancy. And in both cases the voyage may be said to have its ups and downs. The social reality of pregnancy also is embedded in history. Thus, what happens to men and women as they cross the pregnancy divide is, in large part, a function of *when* they make the crossing. Simply stated, what is true today may not have been true yesterday and may not be true tomorrow.

Expectant mothers and expectant fathers experience similar things. Both are likely to be concerned about how the baby will alter their lives. Both are likely to be flushed with pride and a sense of vitality at their ability to procreate. As for differences, expectant mothers in this society are, paradoxically enough, revered *and* scorned, which helps to explain why so many women feel both happy and sad about being pregnant. Expectant fathers, on the other hand, tend to be made fun of or, perhaps worse, ignored altogether; like it or not, they generally must be satisfied with a supporting rather than a starring social role.

Pregnancy not only affects the way husbands and wives think about themselves, it also affects the way they think about and act toward each other. Research indicates that during pregnancy people tend to have less sex with their partners, yet feel closer and more connected to their partners at the same time. Subtle and complex changes in the work and power structure of the home also have been found to take place.

It is a shame that so few sociological studies of pregnancy have been conducted. I suspect that we would know a lot more today about continuity and change in marriage had we focused more on this brief but important phase in the family life cycle.

REVIEW QUESTIONS

(1) What are the salient features of the stages that punctuate the social pregnancy?

(2) How does the social reality of expectant motherhood differ from the social reality of expectant fatherhood? How are they the same?

(3) What effect does pregnancy have on the husband-wife relationship? What changes in a marriage and what does not? Why?

SUGGESTED ASSIGNMENTS

(1) Interview a woman who currently is pregnant. Compare her experience with what was said in this chapter.

(2) Interview a man whose wife is pregnant. Compare his experience with what was said in this chapter.

(3) Choose a decade from the past (for example, the 1940s, 1950s, 1960s) and locate two popular magazine articles on the subject of

pregnancy for that particular decade. See if what was said then would be considered valid today.

NOTE

1. Nine months—or, more accurately, 38 to 42 weeks—is the average gestation period of the human fetus. According to the *Guinness Book of World Records* (McWhirter, 1984), the shortest and longest gestation period among mammals is 12 to 14 days (South American water opossum) and just over 20 months (Asiatic elephant).

CHAPTER
4

Birth

IF YOU HAVE EVER had the opportunity to witness a baby being born, you know what I mean when I say that the physical reality of birth is both an awesome and humbling experience. To think that only seconds before this little person was not even breathing and that nine months earlier he or she did not even exist . . . well, as I said, it is a sight to behold.

But what about the social reality of birth? What can be said about the norms, values, beliefs, and patterns of interaction that surround and, to a certain extent, define the miracle of life? It is this "other reality" of birth—the social reality—that I plan to focus on here.

First, I will review the history and politics of maternity care in America, and then, with the historical-political picture serving as a backdrop, will go on the describe how the three stages in the birth process—labor, parturition, (delivery), and postpartum—are socially constructed as well as physically distinct realities.

THE HISTORY AND POLITICS
OF MATERNITY CARE

Birth in Colonial America

Let us go back to the seventeenth century and peek in at a birth in one of the American colonies—say, Massachusetts.[1] The woman who is about to deliver her first child is 22 years old, and she has been married for 16 months. Her name is Mary. Mary is not in a hospital but in her own bedroom, and she is surrounded by a number of female friends and relatives, whose psychological support she dearly values. Everyone in the room is in a jovial mood, talking and eating. The solidarity that the birth inspires is something that the women look forward to and enjoy.

Mary is undoubtedly the central character in the drama that is unfolding. Everything and everyone is focused on her. There is, however, another important figure, another person whose presence is considered essential. That person is not a doctor, nor is it Mary's husband; during the seventeenth century physicians and fathers-to-be were not expected to assist at childbirth. No, it is a woman who is about 45 years old. It is the midwife.[2]

Having helped to deliver hundreds of babies, the midwife is able to draw on a wealth of experience, and she definitely is deferred to throughout the proceedings. The "tools of her trade" include, among other things, a variety of traditional folk medicines and a collapsible stool that will allow Mary to sit up rather than lie on her back when it comes time to push the baby out.

The midwife believes—and she is correct—that sitting up is a good position for Mary to be in because in this position the baby's head will press against Mary's cervix, opening up the birth passage. If Mary were to lie down, the weight of the baby would press against her spine, which, besides being uncomfortable, is also unhealthy (Rothman, 1982: 81).

Probably the most valuable "tool" that the midwife has brought to this home is her ability to instill confidence in Mary. Seeing herself as someone whose job is not to intervene but to allow nature to take its course, she does whatever she can to facilitate *Mary's delivery of her own baby.* At least, this is the attitude that the birth manuals of the day were encouraging midwives to take. For example,

> The midwife must instruct and comfort the party, not only refreshing her with good meat and drink, but also with sweet words, giving her good hope of a speedy deliverence, encouraging and admonishing her to patience and tolerance, bidding her to hold in her breath so much as she may, also stroking gently with her hands her belly above the navel, for that helps to depress the birth downward [Raynalde, 1626: 97].

After the birth, Mary will "lie in," which means that she will recuperate by staying in bed for three to four weeks while her friends and relatives do her chores and prepare her meals. The women will not be paid for their services, but Mary will give them a dinner party after she recovers. Also, if and when they give birth, they can expect Mary to assist them, and several of the women are, in fact, reciprocating for when Mary helped them recuperate from birth.

In Colonial America, almost everyone assumed that birth was a nonmedical process "owned and operated" by women. The scene just described was thus quite typical (see Wertz and Wertz, 1977: 1-28). However, something would happen in the latter part of the eighteenth century that would transform forever the American way of birth.

The Medicalization of Birth

During Colonial times, America was fairly isolated from the world of medicine. There were no medical schools or hospitals, as there were in Europe, and doctors were not accorded anywhere near the respect that they are given today. However, around 1750 this began to change. More and more American men who aspired to become doctors were going to European medical schools and returning to America to practice. (I say men because women were not permitted to go to medical school.) The infusion of the European-trained doctors' knowledge and skills had a tremendous impact on the health profession in this country. Simply stated, it altered the way that Americans *perceived* the profession. While in Europe, the new doctors had been taught to view the practice of medicine as a science. They had attended classes in anatomy and physiology and, in the French schools in particular, were instructed to think of the body as a machine. When they returned to this country to start their own practices, they made every effort to convince the American public of the value of the scientific approach to health care. For one thing, they genuinely believed in the scientific approach; they honestly felt that using this approach would help people. They also realized that promoting the scientific approach to health care would increase their standing in the community. The more people who saw health care as a science, the more likely they would be to choose European-trained doctors over other practitioners.

You may find it odd to think of physicians having to "sell" their expertise, given the virtual monopoly that doctors have over health care today. But in the absence of any effective licensing program, the doctors of the 1700s were forced to compete with a variety of healers.

Although some of these healers were clearly incompetent, quite a few were very skilled, in spite of their lack of formal education, and posed a real economic threat to the scientifically minded physicians.

What effect did all of this have on the American way of birth? Quite a dramatic effect. The introduction of the scientific approach to health care was the first step in the medicalization of birth. The conception of the body as a machine seemed to give coherence to the reproductive process: "Just as some doctors were speaking of the function of the stomach as if it were a machine with knives and scissors to pulverize food, so the ... [European-trained practioners] spoke of the womb and birth canal as though they formed a mechanical pump that in particular instances was more or less adequate to expel the fetus" (Wertz and Wertz, 1977: 32). Indeed, the new view of birth that the doctors brought back with them probably was the best "medicine" they could offer their patients, for the truth of the matter was that the mechanical model of birth *was* a lot more accurate than other models popular at the time. The fact that birth was so common also explains why the doctors were eager to subsume birth under a scientific mantle. Here was one activity that occurred often enough to provide a modest income. Moreover, they knew that if they performed successfully they might be asked to become the family's regular doctor.

The Debate Over Forceps

The use of the term "performance" to characterize what the doctors did is very appropriate because it accentuates the *active* role that the European-trained physicians played during the delivery itself. If you remember, when I described the approach that Mary's midwife took throughout Mary's birth, I emphasized her *collaborative* stance. Her job, as she saw it, was not to intervene in the birth process but to facilitate the natural sequence of events. The scientific approach to birth, however, implied not only that birth could be understood through rational thought but that it could be controlled through rational action.

Perhaps the best example of the kinds of "rational" action that the European-trained physicians would be inclined to take—and *the* practice that at the time most clearly distinguished male midwifery from female midwifery—was the use of forceps. Invented during the sixteenth or seventeenth century by the barber-surgeon, Peter Chamberlen, *forceps* were a metal instrument resembling two large spoons facing each other. They were designed to be inserted into the birth canal and cupped around the baby's head, and, once applied, would be manipulated in an effort to pull the baby out of the mother's uterus. Forceps were not the first instrument to be used during birth. For centuries a variety of objects (sticks, knives, hooks, and so on) had been employed to remove obstructions or extract dead fetuses. But forceps were the first instrument designed to free the fetus without killing it. Before forceps, an ill-positioned baby often meant that either the baby or the mother or both would die during birth.

Unfortunately, the invention of forceps did not, at least initially, significantly reduce the infant or maternal mortality rate. First of all, Peter Chamberlen and his family kept the invention a secret for over a century. By publicizing only that they knew how to remove an impacted fetus safely, they were able to beat their competitors. Second, the men who were using forceps did not always know how to use them properly. Mechanically extracting a baby by its head involves considerable risk. If you do not know exactly what you are doing, you can crush the baby's skull and cause internal damage to the mother. Although the European-trained doctors may have known more than most about the female anatomy, they still had a lot to learn. Thus, a number of birth-associated fatalities and injuries during Colonial times can be attributed to the improper use of the instrument.

The disagreement between the male and female midwives over the use of forceps centered on *when* they should be used. In other words, at what point in the birth process is it legitimate to attempt a forceps delivery? Although some midwives (both male and female) believed that forceps should never be used, most were of the opinion that forceps could and should be used as a last resort. Male midwives, however, were more likely than female midwives to intervene during the early stages of labor, and some male midwives believed that a forceps delivery was actually safer than a natural birth because it reduced the time that the mother was in labor.

Explaining why male midwives—and especially the European-trained doctors—were more likely than female midwives to rely on forceps requires some understanding of the social reality of American health care during the seventeenth, eighteenth, and nineteenth centuries. You will recall that I referred to the man who invented forceps—Peter Chamberlen—as a barber-surgeon. It may seem strange to put barbers in the same category as surgeons, and stranger still to think of a barber inventing an instrument to help deliver babies, but up until 1745 barbers and surgeons belonged to the same guild or trade union (Starr, 1982: 38), and they, and only they, had the legal right to use surgical instruments. Thus, if for some reason a mother could not naturally deliver her baby, custom dictated that the midwife call in a barber-surgeon to remove the fetus surgically by dismembering it in utero. Midwives, in other words, were not allowed to intervene surgically in the birth process. Given that barber-surgeons were the only ones allowed to do surgery, it is not surprising that a barber-surgeon would be the first to develop forceps. The fact that a man invented forceps is also not surprising, because women were excluded from becoming barber-surgeons and hence also prevented from using surgical instruments (Rothman, 1982: 52-54). Thus, one reason that female midwives were less likely to use forceps is that, under the law, they were not allowed to use them.

The law, however, was not the only thing standing in the way of women using forceps, for even after the law was changed most female midwives refused to use the instrument. The other—perhaps more important—reason that they were less likely to use forceps is that they were committed to a noninterventionist approach. Female midwives failed to see the value of a procedure that, as far as they were concerned, was not only inefficient but also dangerous. One eighteenth-century midwife claimed,

> A few, and very few indeed, of the midwives, dazzled with that vogue into which the instruments brought the men . . . attempted to employ them [but] soon discovered that they were at once insignificant and dangerous substitutes for their own hands, with which they were sure of conducting their operations both more safely, more effectually, and with less pain to the patient [Nihell, 1760: 167n].

Although the female midwives continued to prefer natural childbirth, the male midwives and European-trained doctors were becoming increasingly fond of forceps deliveries and other interventions (for example, using drugs to accelerate labor). First, they believed that artificially controlling the birth process was more in keeping with a scientific approach. As they saw it, their task was to "improve upon" nature by reducing the duration of labor and thus presumably save both the baby and the mother a lot of stress and pain. Rather than allow a mother to deliver her own child, they would deliver the child; they, rather than mothers, would be in charge.

The male midwives and doctors also found the notion of being in control more attractive. Their own sense of professional self-worth seemed to be bolstered by the idea of their having a starring role at each birth. Symbolic of this shift in self-image is the doctors' decision in the late 1820s to drop the title "midwife" in favor of "obstetrician." (Up until this point, obstetrics was known as midwifery, even if it was practiced by a physician and associated with a medical school.) What the doctors were looking for was a title that would distinguish them from their competitors and, at the same time, signify their interventionist approach to birth.

"Obstetrician," which is derived from the Latin term *obstare* meaning "to stand before" was selected because it had the advantage of sounding like other honorable professions, such as "electrician" or "geometrician," in which men variously understood and dominated nature [Wertz and Wertz, 1977: 66].

Last, many midwives and doctors discovered that an interventionist approach was more profitable than a noninterventionist approach. They soon learned that if they allowed nature to take its course, they might be tied up for hours attending to a single birth, but that if they used forceps they could arrive on the scene, quickly deliver the baby, and then move on to other paying customers. Using forceps and other interventions also was more theatrical. The doctors had a sense that they would make a more favorable impression (and ultimately more money) if they appeared to be *doing something* to bring about the delivery. In fact, there is evidence to suggest that some doctors opted for a forceps delivery even when they knew that a woman could naturally deliver her baby because they did not want to look like just another spectator. One consequence of the doctors' flair for the dramatic is that people began to look upon birth as something that could not proceed without intervention. In other words, women— especially middle- and upper-class women—began to believe that if the doctors did not intervene in the birth process something might go wrong: hence, "women may have come to anticipate difficult births whether or not doctors urged that possibility as a means of selling themselves. Having seen the 'best,' perhaps each woman wanted the 'best' for her delivery, whether she needed it or not" (Wertz and Wertz, 1977: 64-65).

The Defeminization of Birth

It was not long before the male midwives and doctors realized that their own financial interests would best be served if they eliminated the competition from the female midwives. Thus, around the beginning of the nineteenth century the male midwives and doctors began to try to discredit the female midwives—either by citing their lack of formal training and adherence to traditional (outdated) methods, or by claiming that midwifery was too crude an occupation for "ladies" to be involved with, or by depicting women as weak and irrational.

Attacking the female midwives on the basis of gender was an ironic twist because when the male midwives and doctors began to practice the fact that they were men was perceived as a distinct disadvantage; people were reluctant to admit men to what had hitherto been a for-women-only event. In 1522, a German physician was burned at the stake for disguising himself as a woman so he could observe a birth (Myles, 1971: 698). However, now the men were saying that women did not have the capacity to be birth attendants. Besides being labeled too emotional, women were said to be constrained by their menstrual cycle—a "periodic infirmity of their sex . . . [which] unfits them for any responsible effort of mind" (Storer, 1868). As one pamphlet put it,

> They [women] have not that power of action, or that active power of mind, which is essential to the practice of a surgeon. They have less power of restraining and governing the natural tendencies to sympathy and are more disposed to yield to the expressions of acute sensibility . . . where they become the principal agents, the feelings of sympathy are too powerful for the cool exercise of judgment" [Anonymous, 1820: 4-6].

Implied in this and virtually every other tirade was the idea that birth attendants must be technicians. Thus, we can see that an interventionist stance toward birth was instrumental in men's efforts to exclude women from midwifery and obstetrics.

Although the men's propaganda was hogwash, pure and simple, people believed it, and in a fairly short period of time—during the period 1800 to 1830—most middle-class and upper-class families shifted their allegiance from female to male birth attendants. (Female midwives continued to assist low-income and immigrant families up to the twentieth century, partly because these families could not afford to retain a male midwife or doctor and partly because many male midwives and doctors preferred middle-income and upper-income patients.) The defeminization of the birth process was given further impetus when doctors began to lobby to exclude all midwives—male as well as female—from the practice of obstetrics. Because women were overtly and covertly barred from admission to many American medical schools, once birth was defined as a medical specialty a number of highly qualified women were prevented from becoming obstetricians.

From Home to Hospital

The medical establishment's control over the birth process did not enter its final stage until the 1900s. You see, all the time the doctors and midwives were arguing over who should tend to maternity cases, one thing remained essentially unchanged: Giving birth was something that women preferred to do at home. To be sure, there were maternity hospitals in America during the eighteenth century, but they primarily were "for poor, homeless, or working-class married women who could not deliver at home but who doctors and philanthropists believed deserved medical treatment and the chance to recuperate in an atmosphere of moral uplift—what lying-in at home was thought to provide for more fortunate women" (Wertz and Wertz, 1977: 132).

The situation was about to change, however. Whereas in 1900 fewer than 5% of American women delivered in hospitals, by 1940 the figure was 50%, and today it is close to 100%.

Why the change? Several factors were involved. The more committed the doctors became to intervention, the more they believed that there was no such thing as a "normal," trouble-free delivery. Having adopted a Murphy's Law attitude toward birth—whatever can go wrong, will go wrong—they came to the conclusion that the safest place to give birth was a hospital because only in a hospital do doctors have the equipment and personnel to "perform" technical deliveries.

Although perceived safety was the main reason behind the obstetricians' advocacy of hospital birth, it was by no means the only reason. The doctors also were attracted to the convenience and prestige that the hospital afforded. It was a lot easier to tend to patients in one central location than it was to visit each house when called, especially when you think of the ever-growing assortment of surgical tools and drugs on which obstetricians relied. Also, it was easier to train students in a hospital setting. Besides being able to assist the doctors, the students would have the opportunity to see a variety of cases "under laboratory conditions." Finally, obstetricians discovered that they had more authority when they worked in a hospital. When they visited people's homes, they often had to defer to the wishes of the families. But in the hospital everyone catered to them.

It would be wrong to conclude that doctors forced mothers to adopt the medical model of birth, because the fact is that women were themselves instrumental in the shift to this model. Women, for example, were the ones who initially pressured doctors to begin using drugs to not only relieve the pain of childbirth but render mothers unconscious during delivery. One procedure that became especially popular as a result of women's efforts was the administration of a drug (scopolamine) that removed from memory the pain that often accompanied birth. The temporary amnesia, known as "twilight sleep," was "eagerly adopted by fashionable women" in the early 1900s, and by the late 1930s had become standard procedure in a number of hospitals (Wertz and Wertz, 1977: 132-152).

The Prepared Childbirth Movement

The medicalization and defeminization of the American birth process were moving full steam ahead when, much to the medical community's surprise, a countermovement arose. Around 1940, women began to question the wisdom of the interventionist approach to birth. Specifically, they began to have doubts about whether using drugs was in the best interest of the baby and whether being made unconscious or oblivious was the best way to experience the wonder of birth.

The countermovement seems to have been caused by two things: advances in medical knowledge and technology and changes in the way women thought about themselves and their roles.

Once the fear of death traditionally associated with childbirth was removed by medical advances, women began to regard birth more positively. Now that medicine could anticipate abnormality, prevent it, and usually overcome it, fewer women and children died in birth; women regarded nature itself, therefore, as more reliable and began to wonder whether medical treatment was necessary and safe. [Also] after World War II both popular psychology and a reemphasis on domesticity encouraged women to believe once again that motherhood was a woman's fundamental purpose; she therefore should be awake to experience its sublime beginning [Wertz and Wertz, 1977: 178-179].

The new attitude toward birth took a variety of forms. Initially, the philosophy was that birth was painful primarily because women had been taught to fear birth; if mothers could be taught to relax, they would experience little, if any, pain. Thus, in his book *Childbirth Without Fear* (1944) Grantly Dick-Read, a British obstetrician, emphasized the importance of practicing relaxation techniques during pregnancy and then using those relaxation techniques rather than pain-alleviating drugs during labor and delivery. Later, a French obstetrician introduced a method that relied not on relaxation but on conditioning. In his book *Painless Childbirth* (1956) Ferdinand Lamaze contended that if mothers could condition their brains not to interpret certain physiological stimuli as pain, then no pain would be felt. The key again was preparation, but instead of practicing relaxation techniques, women were instructed to rely on concentration activities (for example, deep breathing and panting) that would send countersignals to the brain stronger than the pain signals it would receive during labor and delivery.

The Lamaze method proved to be more popular than the Dick-Read method because of its accent on female autonomy. Many women felt that under the Lamaze method they were regaining control of the birth process. In their minds, *they* rather than the doctors would be the ones who delivered their babies.

Although women may have felt that they were regaining control of the birth process under the Lamaze method, the truth is that under this method and practically every other prepared-childbirth method they were still allowing doctors to dictate what women should do. Note that I referred to the Lamaze method as a *prepared-childbirth* method, not a *natural-childbirth* method. In reality, the Lamaze and Dick-Read methods prepare women for the problems they will encounter in a medically managed birth. Thus, these methods are not in the same category as a natural or noninterventionist birth; rather, they are a type of medical or interventionist birth.

Another way to look at it is that over the years women have had three kinds of birth experiences (Rothman, 1982: 174-178). For most of human history, women collaborated with their birth attendants in a spirit of *mutual participation*. The early midwives, as noted, saw themselves as facilitators; they helped women to deliver their own babies. But with the advent of the medical or interventionist approach to birth, women increasingly found themselves in an *active-passive relationship*, whereby doctors, often as a first resort, would use forceps, surgery, or drugs to remove ("deliver") the child of an unconscious mother. Grantly Dick-Read and Ferdinand Lamaze certainly deserve credit for publicizing the drawbacks of an active-passive birth relationship, but neither of them advocated a return to mutual participation. No, what they did essentially is propose a third kind of birth experience, one of *guidance-cooperation*. Whereas the active-passive model casts doctors as "mechanics" responsible for running and sometimes repairing the reproductive "machine," the guidance-cooperation model encouraged doctors to be counselors or coaches. As for the women who were having the babies, they were told to be good *patients* by cooperating and listening to their physicians. In other words, the active-passive model and the guidance-cooperation model operate on the assumption that expectant women and new mothers are ill and that doctors should be the ultimate authorities during pregnancy, labor, and delivery; and both models take for granted the validity of a medical, typically hospital-based birth (Nash and Nash, 1979; Rothman, 1982).

The Natural Childbirth Movement

Recently, there has emerged a new challenge to the medical model. An increasing number of women now are choosing to have their babies outside the hospital, either in their homes or in what have become known as "birthing centers." What is more, they are choosing not to rely on a variety of procedures that have become almost commonplace in hospital births. I am referring to ultrasound monitoring (an X-ray process that allows you to see your baby in utero), fetal electrocardiograms (heart rate measurement), and episiotomies (cutting a woman's perineum during delivery).

The underlying theme of the natural childbirth movement (as it is called) is the belief that birth is not a medical-technological phenomenon and that the ones who are having the babies—the mothers, but to some degree the fathers, too—deserve to be on an equal, if not higher, footing with their birth attendants, whether they be midwives or doctors. What is being advanced, in other words, is a return to the mutual-participation model of birth.

The American College of Obstetrics and Gynecology believes that the natural-childbirth movement is not only anachronistic but also dangerous (Findlay, 1985). The attitude of the College is as follows: Suppose complications arise during labor (for example, the baby's heart rate unexpectedly drops) and the mother is not in a modern hospital with its available staff and equipment; what then? Natural-childbirth proponents contend that fewer than 10% of all births actually require medical intervention to ensure the safety of the baby or mother and that, more often than not, women who are going to experience complicated births can be identified beforehand (that is, during pregnancy).

The controversy over the best place to give birth is extremely complex. If we compare the neonatal mortality rate for hospital and nonhospital births, we find that babies delivered in a hospital are less likely to die during birth than babies delivered outside a hospital. However, this comparison is confounded by (among other things) the fact that a higher proportion of nonhospital births are unplanned (for example, on the way to the hospital, a woman gives birth in the car). If we control for planning status and compare hospital births and *planned* nonhospital births, we find the neonatal mortality rate in the two settings to be about the same (Hinds et al., 1985).

The natural-childbirth movement is a call for more planned non-hospital births—births that take place in a home or birthing center and are monitored by a trained midwife or obstetrician. It is *not* a call for a return to the times when delivering babies was more of an art than a science. Right now, however, we do not know enough about the risks associated with planned nonhospital births. This is one area in which systematic research is sorely needed.

STAGES IN THE BIRTH PROCESS

I have provided a fairly detailed description of the history and politics of maternity care to help you to better understand the interpersonal dynamics that characterize contemporary birth experiences. The fact is that the antithetical forces that have struggled to shape obstetrical practice in the past continue to have an impact on obstetrical practice today (McBride, 1982: 413). Thus, every birth in America—no matter what the *modus operandi*—is a combination of the medical and natural perspectives. This is most obvious in a prepared (for example, Lamaze) birth. However, it is also true in a birth in which there is a considerable amount of medical intervention or one in which there is no medical intervention whatsoever, for each of these "pure" types is socially meaningful only when compared with the other.

Up to now, I have described the birth process almost as if it were an unbroken line extending from pregnancy to parenthood, but in actuality there are at least three distinct stages that mark the transition: labor, parturition, and postpartum.

Labor

Physically speaking, an expectant woman is said to be in labor when her uterus begins to contract rhythmically and the baby begins to move through the opening between the uterus and vagina, called the cervix. At one time it was thought that it was best if labor began after the ninth month of pregnancy (about 40 weeks) or, if not then, during the seventh month. But today most medical experts agree that it is best if labor begins around the 38th to the 42nd week (Kay, 1982: 14).

It is possible for an expectant mother to feel as if she is in labor when in fact she is not. True labor and false labor are usually distinguishable to someone who is trained to know the difference, but there have been times when even the most experienced physician, midwife, or mother has been fooled.

The power to interpret the signs of labor and to decide if and when delivery is imminent is an issue that graphically illustrates the contemporary conflict between the medical and natural perspectives. For example, suppose a woman, whom we will assume has decided to have her baby in a hospital, is close to her due date and begins to experience contractions that she believes are genuine. She may drive or be driven to the hospital with the intention of admitting herself to the maternity ward, but the fact is that she must *be admitted* by the hospital staff: "The state of being in labor, like illness or any deviance, is an ascribed status: that is, it is a position to which a person is assigned by those in authority" (Rothman, 1982: 166). One of the first things the staff (the authorities) will determine is whether or not the woman's cervix is dilated. If it is not, the staff may very well conclude that the woman is not "really" in labor or that her labor is not far enough along to warrant admitting her. In either case, the woman probably will be told to go home, at least for the present. If the women complies with the staff's wishes then, despite her *physical* sensations, she is not in labor; that is, she does not occupy the *social* position of "woman in labor." If, however, she is able to convince the staff to admit her, then she will be treated as if she is in labor—she will, for instance, be escorted to a labor room—even if her cervix does not begin to dilate for, say, 24 hours and she does not have her baby until 12 hours after that. In this latter situation, her medical records will indicate a 36-hour labor, which is a poorly managed birth from the hospital's point of view (Rothman, 1982: 165-167).

Of course, throughout history expectant women have considered it important to be able to determine when their babies would arrive, but with the shift from homes to hospitals the timing of the onset and progress of labor has become paramount. A lot of it has to do with the fact that a hospital's scarce resources (there are only so many maternity rooms and so on), when pitted against the demands of a fertile population, necessitate the *scheduling* (that is, social clocking and synchronization) of labor and deliveries (Kovit, 1972). In other words, from the hospital administrator's point of view, if *every* mother were allowed to proceed at her own speed toward delivery, a hospital's staff would periodically find itself taxed beyond its limits.

Critics of hospital birth contend that scheduling and clock watching in general are "basic to the medical management of birth."

> They [time tables] provide a way of structuring and a justification for controlling what is happening. By setting up ideas of what "on time" means—whether for due dates or length of a particular stage of labor— medicine also sets up the occasions for medical intervention to bring women back on schedule [Rothman, 1982: 255].

What about the father; what is he doing while his wife is in labor? In Colonial times he typically had the responsibility of summoning the midwife to his home and then keeping pretty much out of the way. Twenty years ago his job primarily was to drive his wife to the hospital and then dispatch himself to a waiting room until a nurse came and told him that the birth was over and that he was welcome to visit his son or daughter in the nursery. Today, however, a husband is likely to be present during labor, comforting and—in the case of prepared child-birth—"coaching" or "supervising" his wife.

The degree to which fathers now have become involved—often to the point of breathing and panting in unison with their wives—is reminiscent of the couvade rituals that anthropologists discovered in their cross-cultural studies (Rothman, 1982: 99-100). *Couvade* is derived from the French term *couver*, meaning "to sit on" or "to hatch." It refers to the custom whereby the father figuratively "substitutes himself for the mother when labor begins" (Milinaire, 1974: 285). The specifics vary from one society to the next, but generally what happens is that "the man goes to bed sobbingly, writhes with ostensible pains, moans, has warm compresses applied to his body, has himself nursed attentively, and submits to dietary restrictions for days, weeks, or, in exceptional cases, even for months" (Diner, 1981: 86). Scholars believe that couvade rituals function to communicate the husband's right to the child and validate his role as the father (Bachofen, 1967). Perhaps the rituals of today's husband-coached childbirth do the same thing.

Parturition

Parturition is the second stage in the birth process. It begins when the cervix is fully dilated (10 centimeters) and ends, from minutes to hours later, with delivery of the child. If you have had a baby yourself and opted for a prepared childbirth, you will remember parturition as the time when you were told to use your abdominal muscles to push the baby out.

Again, although birth is a biological metamorphosis, it occurs within a sociological context. Thus, as was the case with labor, the state of being in parturition is a position to which a person is assigned by the powers that be. This is especially apparent in hospitals that spatially separate women in labor and women in parturition.

Since a woman will be moved from one room to another to mark the transition from one stage [to the next], the professional staff has to make a distinction between laboring and delivering, and then apply that distinction to the individual woman. A cut-off point has to be established at which a woman is no longer viewed as laboring but as delivering. If the point is missed, and the woman delivers, say, in the hall on the way to the delivery room, then she is seen as having "precipped," having had a precipitous delivery. If the point is called too soon, if the staff decides that the woman is ready to deliver and the physical reality is that she has another hour to go, then the concern is aroused about the length of the second stage, because she has spent that extra hour in a delivery rather than a labor room [Rothman, 1982: 168-169].

The social reality of the delivery room is different than that of the labor room. The difference is akin to the feeling you might have when you are in an airport and are called to get on the plane. All things up to that point—planning the trip, buying the tickets, getting to the gate, and waiting at the gate—are nothing more than precursors to the main event—that is, taking off. The same is true when it comes to having a baby. Deciding to have a child, conceiving the child, going through pregnancy, and experiencing labor are viewed as steps or, in some people's minds, obstacles to the birth itself. Thus, there is a sense of relief, of "having arrived," when the time comes to be wheeled into the delivery room.[3]

According to one participant observation study, the parturition stage itself is composed of three social substages: patient introduction, baby announcement, and "I'm done—Congratulations" (Kovit, 1972).

During the *patient introduction* substage, the mother-to-be is introduced to those in the room whom she has not yet met and invariably told, regardless of her actual condition, that she is "doing fine" and "will be all right." Two other popular refrains are "the worst is over" and "it won't be long now."

Unlike her seventeenth-century counterpart, the parturient mother will not be situated on a birthing stool; rather, she will rest flat on her back strapped to a delivery table with her feet up in stirrups (metal heel supports attached to the table), or she will lie in a bed that is designed to prop her back up at about a 45-degree angle. The advantage of today's delivery positions is that they give the obstetrician a clear view of the mother's vaginal area and make it easier for him or her to use forceps in the event of a difficult birth and to cut the perineum surgically rather than allowing it to tear when the baby comes. The disadvantage of these positions, ironically enough, is that because of how the birth canal is designed the baby must be pushed or pulled upwards, increasing the likelihood that forceps will be seen as a necessary alternative. Also, a lot of pressure is placed on the perineum, increasing the likelihood that it will tear or need to be cut (Rothman, 1982: 81, 254).

The *baby announcement* substage begins when the crown of the baby's head starts to show ("I see it!") and ends with the assessment of the baby's condition ("He's got all his parts"). In between is the long-awaited gender proclamation ("It's a boy/girl!").

Barring an emergency, a mother who has opted for a natural or prepared childbirth can look forward to being awake during the delivery. A mother who has chosen a medicated childbirth can also anticipate being awake if her doctor administers a local rather than a general anesthetic. Being awake does not necessarily mean that the mother will actually see her baby being born. It is anatomically impossible for her to see the crown of the baby's head as it starts to come out. A mirror is sometimes used to allow the mother to catch a glimpse of her newborn, but even this is not totally satisfactory, as anyone who drives a car knows.

The fact that the mother has the worst view of the birth increases her dependency on others (the staff, her husband) to *tell* her what the baby looks like. In her efforts to get an accurate picture of the baby's condition she is likely to be sensitive not only to what others say but also to how they say it.

Most of the time her hunger for information and anxiety over whether she is being told the truth will be short-lived. During the delivery itself she may wonder if everything is okay. But immediately after the delivery she will be shown and perhaps handed the baby and will be able to see for herself whether or not the baby has all its fingers and toes, and so on. Next, the baby will be whisked to a side table to be weighed and evaluated, and again the mother will anxiously listen to the nurses' assessment of the baby's heart rate, respiratory rate, and muscle tone. But within minutes the baby will be back and the mother will again have the chance to determine firsthand whether or not she has delivered a healthy child.

What if the baby is not okay; what then? As you would surmise, the social reality of the birth announcement substage changes dramatically if there is something wrong with the child. Here, for example, is how one mother described what it was like to give birth to a Down's syndrome (mongoloid) child:

> I remember very vividly. The doctor did not say anything at all when the baby was born. Then he said, "It's a boy," and the way he hesitated, I immediately said, "Is he all right?" And he said, "He has ten fingers and ten toes," so in the back of my mind I knew there was something wrong [Darling, 1979: 129].

Although her doctor knew at birth that the baby was not normal, he did not communicate this information to the mother until the next day. The mother, however, read between the lines and knew from the beginning that all was not well.

Sometimes a baby will be stillborn (that is, dead at birth). The pregnancy may have been uneventful, the labor progressing on schedule, and then—without warning—the fetus may stop moving and no heartbeat can be heard. As is the case when a child is born with a birth defect, the atmosphere in the room changes markedly during and after the birth of a stillborn child. One of my students whose son was strangled by his own umbilical cord specifically remembered how quiet everyone became once it was learned that the child was dead, and how the staff avoided talking about the baby. The doctors and nurses seemed to assume that by minimizing what had happened (for example, by saying things like, "Don't worry, you can get pregnant again") they were helping the couple. The problem was, however, this particular husband and wife *wanted* to talk about their son; they wanted to be treated as *parents* whose child had died.

Studies of the social reality of newborn death indicate that the attitude of this couple is not unusual (see Peppers and Knapp, 1980). It appears that many, if not most, men and women who have suffered through the birth of a stillborn child prefer to think of the dead infant as a member of the family. In light of these studies, hospitals increasingly are adopting policies that encourage parents not only to hold their stillborn babies soon after they are delivered but to photograph them as well.

The third substage of parturition is *"I'm done—Congratulations."* During this stage, the staff tells the mother that she is "done" and that she "did a good job" ("That's a beautiful boy you got there; nice work"). Interestingly enough, the staff's comments may have little relation to what they really believe. In the participant observation study, "Patients who acted atrociously from the staff's perspective were told the same thing [as the patients who acted 'correctly']. Babies called cute in the delivery room in the presence of the mother were often called other things when the mother was out of earshot" (Kovit, 1972: 21). As I indicated earlier, because a mother is supersensitive both to what the doctors and nurses say and to how they say it, we can assume that there are numerous instances in which the staff erroneously believes that they have successfully masked their true feelings.

Although the boundaries of the patient introduction and baby announcement substages are relatively clear, the boundaries of "I'm done—Congratulations" are somewhat vague. The "I'm done—Congratulations" substage continues not only after the woman is brought to the recovery room—an area where mothers are monitored (for vital signs and so on) before being transported to the maternity ward—but also for the whole time that she is in the hospital. And even after she goes home, she will be congratulated by friends and relatives "for a job well done." Thus, it is perhaps more accurate to say that the "I'm done— Congratulations" phase begins during parturition and ends during the final stage in the birth process, commonly called postpartum.

Postpartum

The word *postpartum* means "period following parturition." In medicine, it is defined as "the [six-week] period beginning immediately after delivery and ending when the woman's body has returned as nearly as possible to its prepregnant state" (Miller and Brooten, 1983: 383). In this book, however, postpartum is limited to the time that the mother is in the hospital. The reason is that, although a woman's physical condition may not change the day she leaves the hospital, her social condition most certainly does, and because it is the social reality of becoming a parent that is of interest here, abiding by the medical definition of postpartum would be misleading.

There are several things that make the postpartum stage noteworthy. First, there is the fact that although the baby belongs to the parents, responsibility for the baby's care resides with the hospital staff. Thus, for example, it generally is not the parents but the doctors and nurses who decide what and when the baby will be fed and who will be allowed to visit. Even on the day the mother leaves the hospital, the nurses will insist on carrying the baby to the car and placing him or her in the car. It is only after the baby has been transported to another site—the car—that the hospital's caretaking responsibilities end. In one respect, it is nice to have the ever-present and knowledgeable staff telling you what to do. Caring for a baby requires a lot of skill, and most parents welcome whatever help they can get. On the other hand, however, it is odd to have to ask permission to touch or even to see your own baby.

Another aspect of the postpartum stage is the physical segregation of the child and mother. Typically, in a hospital newborns are kept in a nursery and periodically (every three or four hours) brought to their mothers in the maternity ward to be fed and nurtured. This separation is in keeping with the medical view that babies and mothers have distinct and sometimes conflicting needs. Babies need "care." Mothers need "rest." Babies cannot get adequate care from their mothers because the mothers are resting, and mothers cannot get adequate rest if they have to tend to their babies. Interestingly enough, what seems at first glance to be a commonsense way to handle a tough situation is viewed by some as but another example of unnecessary intervention on the part of doctors. For example, whereas doctors conceptually separate infants and expectant and new mothers—and have even developed distinct medical specialties for each group (namely pediatrics and obstetrics)—natural-childbirth proponents view infants and mothers as interdependent. In the natural-childbirth model,

> The mother's need for rest is defined as the need to be freed from everything but herself and her baby. The infant's needs are perceived as body contact, colostrum, and then milk. Far from being contradictory, these needs, it is believed, all come together as the mother lies in bed, dozing and nursing her baby [Rothman, 1982: 184].

Some doctors and hospitals have begun to see the value of this approach. Whereas before a mother would not be allowed to hold her baby until she was moved and had "rested," today it is not uncommon for a mother to be given her child while in the recovery room. We know now that a newborn will be more awake and attentive during the first hour or so after birth than at any other time within the first 24 hours, and many parents (and babies) get tremendous satisfaction from this early contact. Also, some hospitals have changed their rules, such that they now permit "rooming in," which means that instead of staying in the nursery, the baby is kept in a crib alongside the mother's bed. There may even be an extra bed for the father, so that the family will not be broken up when visiting hours are over.

BIRTH BY CESAREAN SECTION

If there are indications that a mother and/or baby will not survive a vaginal birth or that either will be physically traumatized by the experience (for example, a mother may hemorrhage during labor or the fetus may be improperly aligned in the birth canal), then a cesarean section may be performed. A *cesarean section* (C-section) is a surgical operation in which an incision is made in the mother's abdomen and the baby literally is pulled from the mother's womb.

Myth has it that the name of the operation derives from the fact that Julius Caesar was born by cesarean section, but the truth is that the infamous Roman emperor was delivered vaginally. More likely, the term comes from the seventh-century (B.C.) Roman decree that if a woman died while she was pregnant, the child was immediately to be cut from her abdomen in order to be saved. Originally the dictum was part of the *Lex Regia*, but later it was incorporated into the *Lex Caesare*, hence the association between Caesar and the operation (Sorel, 1984: 109-110).

Note that initially the operation was sanctioned *only* in the event that the mother was already dead. Performing a C-section on a healthy mother was out of the question in ancient Rome. Given the state of medical knowledge then, such an operation would surely have resulted in the mother's death.

Although there is evidence to suggest that C-sections on live mothers were attempted periodically throughout history, apparently the first successful cesarean operation was not performed until the year 1500. Jacob Nufer, a Swiss sow-gelder (someone whose job it is to castrate pigs) is said, so the story goes, to have saved both his wife and his child after thirteen midwives had tried and failed to maneuver the baby through the vagina. And the first successful C-section in America did not take place until 1793, when a Virginia doctor by the name of Jesse Bennett performed the operation on his wife (Sorel, 1984: 111-112).

The maternal mortality rate following C-sections continued to be high up to the end of the nineteenth century (92% of the mothers who underwent the operation in New York City in 1887 died). What turned things around was a book published in 1882, a book in which a German physician, one Max Sanger, contended that during a C-section it was crucial to treat not only the abdominal wound but the uterine (that is, internal) wound as well. Sanger also advocated the use of buried sutures to close the wound (Burchell, 1981).

Although medical advances have contributed to making a cesarean section a safer operation (for example, we now have more sophisticated antibiotics and anesthesia), the fact still remains that a C-section *is an operation*, and all operations entail some amount of risk. This is why some people are concerned about the recent increase in the rate of cesarean births.

Perhaps chief among the complaints against hospitals is the alarming rise of cesarean-section deliveries. In 1970, C-sections accounted for just 5.5

percent of all U.S. births; by 1978, that number jumped to 15.2 percent; by 1982, to 18.5 percent. To some extent, that increase may be due to a rising older-mother population who are higher-risk patients, but the proportion of those mothers by no means explains the change entirely. While some doctors believe the C-section rate is leveling off, many critics remain skeptical, contending that, over the past decade, a generation of doctors has been trained who have rarely seen a difficult vaginal delivery. Those doctors, some critics charge, order surgery at the earliest appearance of a problem in labor including births that are progressing too slowly and are, therefore, disrupting the doctor's own schedule. Doctors may also do C-sections to avoid the complications that could precipitate malpractice suits [Warshaw, 1984: 50].

In reply, doctors first point to the fact that many babies and mothers have been saved by C-sections, and that many children who would have suffered irreparable brain damage had they been born vaginally are living healthy, normal lives, thanks to the operation. Second, they note that it is true that some C-sections are unnecessary, but that one generally cannot tell which C-section children could have been delivered vaginally until *after* the birth. In other words, the physicians argue that it is better to perform an unnecessary C-section than to hope that a potentially risky vaginal delivery will be successful.

There are some obstetricians who feel that, if anything, doctors often wait too long before deciding to do a C-section and that many of the complications associated with the operation could be avoided if it were scheduled in advance (before women went into labor). The obstetricians who hold this view primarily are concerned about the risks associated with performing emergency C-sections on women who are postterm (that is, past 40 weeks gestation) and are not advocating that all births be done by cesarean section (Feldman and Freiman, 1985).

The social reality of a C-section birth is different than that of a vaginal birth. If a C-section is unanticipated, it may come at the end of a very long but unsuccessful labor. Thus rather than spending, say, six hours in labor and being rewarded for one's "work" with a vaginal birth, the C-section mother may spend twelve or eighteen hours in labor and then be told that her efforts were not enough. Sadly, it is not unusual for C-section mothers to feel that they have *personally failed.* If a C-section is anticipated (for example, a woman is told early that her birth canal is too small to accommodate a vaginal birth), then the likelihood is that the first stage in the birth process—labor—will be bypassed altogether. Thus, rather than waiting anxiously to go into the labor, the woman may simply be asked to choose her baby's birth date. Some C-section mothers feel that removing the element of surprise takes away something important from the birth experience.

The social reality of the second stage in the birth process—parturition—also is different during a C-section. C-sections are performed in an operating room rather than a delivery or birthing room. Most hospital maternity wards have operating rooms to deal with such emergencies, so the mother probably will not be carted to another wing or floor of the hospital. But the ambience of her surroundings will be different. For one thing, there will be more medical personnel in the room. Second, depending on the hospital, the father may or may not be permitted to watch the birth. It was not too long ago that having a C-section automatically meant that the father could not be present, but more and more hospitals now are allowing dads to witness (and photograph) C-section births. Third, in a vaginal birth, one can debate who gets credit for delivering the baby—the mother or doctor or midwife? However, in a C-section birth, there is no doubt who delivers—the doctor does. Thus, the congratulations that often are offered to a mother in labor for "doing a good job" may not be extended to a mother undergoing a C-section. (Of course, the mother and father will still be praised for having "a beautiful child.")

What about the social reality of the last stage in the birth process—postpartum? Is it also different for a C-section? Yes, it is. A mother's recovery period is likely to be longer and more difficult after a C-section. Whereas a mother who has had a vaginal birth may leave the hospital in one or two days, a mother who has undergone a C-section may be required to stay as long as a week. Also, afterward a mother who has undergone a C-section typically will have more difficulty sleeping and walking and will experience more pain than a woman who has had a vaginal birth. Finally, C-section births are more expensive than vaginal births (Entwisle and Doering, 1981: 109-110).

CONCLUSION

The American way of birth has changed considerably since Colonial times. Four hundred years ago women gave birth at home. Today, the vast majority give birth in a hospital. Four hundred years ago, labor, parturition, and postpartum took place in the company of female friends and relatives. Today, women in the throes of becoming parents are surrounded mainly by strangers, some of whom are men. Also, what was once an event almost totally controlled by nature has increasingly become a procedure subject to medical science and technology: Both the physical and social reality of birth today are governed largely by obstetricians. Finally, birth is a lot safer now than it was then. In Colonial times as many as 1 out of 20 women died during childbirth. Today, only 9 women in 100,000 die giving birth (Demos, 1970; Pritchard et al., 1984).

These historical changes provide a backdrop for understanding some of the battles currently being waged in the field of maternity care. The conflict among proponents of various birth practices essentially is a continuation of a power struggle that has been going on for centuries.

The object of this chapter has been to show how change at the macro-level (for example, the stages in the medicalization of birth) and change at the micro-level (for example, the stages in the birth process) are inextricably linked. As I indicated in the first chapter, we cannot comprehend what it means to become a parent without taking into account the passage of time. Simply stated, social reality—in all its manifestations—is, and always will be, a historical reality.

REVIEW QUESTIONS

(1) What was the typical American birth like back in the seventeenth century?

(2) What factors contributed to the medicalization and defeminization of birth?

(3) What is the difference between a medically managed childbirth and a natural childbirth, and why is prepared childbirth (for example, Lamaze) considered to be more "medical" than "natural"?

(4) What are key features of the social reality of labor, parturition, and delivery?

(5) What are the advantages and disadvantages of having a child by cesarean section?

SUGGESTED ASSIGNMENTS

(1) Interview a midwife and an obstetrician in order to learn how they view their professions, the birth process, and expectant and new parents.

(2) Talk to two women, one who gave birth during the 1940s and another who gave birth sometime in the past year, and identify the similarities and differences in their experiences.

(3) Locate two men whose wives are pregnant and ask them what they intend to do during the birth. If possible, interview them after the birth to see if their expectations about what would happen were realized.

(4) Visit a hospital obstetric ward and observe how labor, parturition, and postpartum are spatially and temporally organized.

NOTES

1. This chapter is based primarily on two excellent books on the sociology of birth: Richard W. Wertz and Dorothy C. Wertz, *Lying In: A History of Childbirth in America* (1977); and Barbara Katz Rothman, *In Labor: Women and Power in the Birthplace* (1982).

2. *Midwife* is a middle English title meaning "with woman."

3. Most women who deliver in a hospital will labor in one room and deliver in another. Some hospitals, however, have begun to allow women to labor and deliver in the same room.

CHAPTER

5

Infant Care

SUPPOSE YOU WERE HANDED an egg, purchased at the grocery store, and told to care for it for, say, a month. By "care" for it, I do not mean that you can put it in your refrigerator and forget about it, but that you have to carry it with you wherever you go. Because an egg will "die" if it is not refrigerated, you will have to devise some way of keeping it cool while you are toting it around. A portable cooler might work, but do not forget that periodically you will have to "feed" ice to your egg. Maybe a battery-powered freezer, which you could sling on your back, would be even better; then all you would have to do is "feed" a battery to your egg every now and then. Remember, an egg is fragile. No matter how you decide to keep it cool, you will have to figure out some way to keep it from cracking. An egg also likes to be cradled, which is why egg cartons are made the way they are, so it might be a good idea to design a little cocoon for your egg. Because you will be on the go a lot—I certainly do not expect you to stay home for a month—you probably should come up with a design that will allow your egg to survive high speeds and sudden stops. You really cannot be too careful when it comes to transporting your egg. A jar could prove fatal—and messy.

This exercise may seem ridiculous, but it is one that often is used by teachers to convey what it is like to care for a baby. Typically, the exercise lasts a week as opposed to a month and almost always the egg (dyed blue or pink for "boy" or "girl") is hard-boiled rather than raw.

86

Nonetheless, students generally return from their week of egg-sitting with a greater sensitivity to what it means to be a parent. This chapter outlines the rights and duties of new parenthood. More specifically, it describes the social organization of families with infants. I will focus on the nature of infant care—what it entails, essentially—and review the factors that account for differences in infant care between one family and the next. I then will discuss the division of labor in families with infants—that is, the quantity and quality of fathering and mothering—and analyze the various theories that have been offered to explain why fathers do so little and mothers do so much.

THE NATURE OF INFANT CARE

The Helplessness of the Human Infant

Most invertebrates and cold-blooded animals reproduce many offspring per pregnancy, whereas most warm-blooded animals reproduce comparatively few. A spawning codfish, for example, lays a million eggs after each gestation, but a human female typically bears only one child at a time.

Which reproductive strategy will characterize a given species depends on its genetic makeup and ecology. A species whose behavior is entirely or almost entirely genetically programmed and whose defense against predators is extremely weak or nonexistent will employ the first strategy, whereas a species whose dependence on learning is strong and whose survival at birth is less contingent on predation than on immunity to illness will employ the second.

The two strategies actually are poles on a continuum rather than discrete either/or dichotomies. Thus, if the first strategy is said to occupy the left pole of the continuum and the second is said to occupy the right, we would find oysters to the left of mice, and mice to the left of elephants; and, more often than not, we would find smaller animals to the left of larger animals (Barash, 1977: 180-183).

The reason that I am telling you about how mice and elephants and codfish reproduce is to introduce the idea that the rights and duties associated with being a parent are partially a function of biology and ecology. Being the father or mother of a human infant means being responsible for a creature that is totally dependent on others. Unlike codfish, which can fend for themselves immediately upon being born,

humans are incapable of surviving after birth unless they are cared
for. In fact, no other neonate requires as much care as the human
neonate does.

How helpless is a newborn baby? An infant has a sucking reflex, so it
does not have to be taught how to nurse. But unless someone puts a
breast or bottle to the baby's mouth, it will die; it cannot find food on its
own. A baby also cannot sit up, let alone walk, and its head will flop back
and forth if it is unsupported. As for growing up to be a healthy, normal
adult, if it is not picked up and cuddled when it is young, and if it is not
taught how to speak and to role play, it will never become a full-fledged
member of society (McCall, 1979).

In a word, babies are demanding, which brings me to the first point I
want to make about the nature of infant care. What makes the
transition to parenthood unique, and for some parents especially
frustrating, is the amount of attention that infants require. Everyone
needs some attention; we all like to be talked to and listened to, and we
all need a little cuddling every now and then. But for the most part, we
can make it on our own. Not infants; they need to be talked to, listened
to, cuddled, fed, cleaned, carried, rocked, burped, soothed, put to
sleep, taken to the doctor, and so on. It seems that there is always
something that new parents have to do, always something to keep them
focused on their relatively helpless charges rather than on themselves.

The Scarcity of Private Time

Given what I have just said, it is hardly surprising that one of the most
common complaints of new parents is that they never seem to have any
time when they can do what they want to do as opposed to what their
babies want them to do (Harriman, 1983; Hobbs, 1965; Hobbs and
Wimbish, 1977).

But what are parents really complaining about when they say that
their babies are time consuming? Essentially, they are bemoaning the
fact that they have to be so accessible to their little ones. Accessibility is
what distinguishes *public time*—time when you are available to
others—and *private time*—time when you are available only to yourself
(Zerubavel, 1981). Thus, what new parents are complaining about is
their lack of privacy.

Interaction in the adult world is characterized by a series of
movements along the accessibility dimension. You are on your way to
lunch and one of your friends stops you to ask a question. Do you want
to talk to him or her; that is, be accessible? Maybe you are so hungry

that you feel that you cannot delay eating another minute, so you tell your friend that you will speak to him or her later; or you suggest that, rather than keep you from eating, your friend join you.

Note that your decision concerning what to do about your friend hinges on the assumption that your friend understands that you want to go to lunch. You assume that he or she can empathize with the fact that you are hungry, and you assume that you can communicate what you intend to do and why. But suppose your friend did not understand you. Suppose not only that he or she did not speak your language but that he or she also was incapable of comprehending hunger—or past, present, and future (as in, "I'll talk to you *later*"). How successful would you then be in carrying out your intentions?

Infants can communicate (by crying, by eye contact, and so on) but they cannot hold a conversation. ("Infant" is derived from the Latin word *infans*, which means incapable of speech.) And they do not understand hunger the way you and I do. Infants, of course, know when they are hungry, but they do not have a concept of hunger; hence, they are incapable of comprehending that you might be hungry. Infants also have yet to learn about the past, the present, and the future (which, by the way, are arbitrary designations), and they certainly do not know what it means to wait or why they should have to wait.

Now suppose that you are home alone with a baby, and you are just about to eat dinner when it begins to cry. Do you cater to yourself or to your baby? Suppose the baby has a dirty diaper and is uncomfortable, but your dinner will get cold if you stop to change it? Do you tell the baby to be patient, that you will change it after you eat? But the baby does not understand what it means to be patient; all it knows is that it is uncomfortable. What do you do? Now imagine episodes like this occurring hundreds of times a week and you have some idea why new parents complain about the scarcity of their private time.

The Problem of Continuous Coverage

Accessibility is a useful notion for comprehending what it means to be a new parent because it helps us to see that the experience of new parents is only a variation on what people have to contend with every day. The "on your way to lunch when stopped by a friend" story was intended to demonstrate this point, but it only hints at how the social organization of a family changes when there is a baby in the house.

Most of our understanding of the dynamics of accessibility and inaccessibility in social life comes not from a study of families but from a study of hospitals. In that study a fairly simple but theoretically powerful idea was advanced, namely that in order for a hospital to carry out its main function, which is patient care, it must be accessible to the community it serves "regardless of the time of the day, the day of the week, or the time of the year." In other words, in order to "provide medical and nursing coverage on a continuous basis" a hospital "must *always* be open" (Zerubavel, 1979: 40).

The responsibilities of *continuous coverage* (round-the-clock care) make it necessary for a hospital to divide its staff into three rotating shifts. Thus, when the morning shift is *on duty* (accessible to the patients), the evening and night shifts are *off duty* (inaccessible to the patients), and vice versa. Some members of the staff—mainly doctors—at any given time will be neither on duty nor off duty but *on call*, which puts them somewhere in the middle as far as accessibility goes.

If we were to examine the inner workings of a hospital, we would actually find that "on duty," "off duty," and "on call" are but three of the many points on the accessibility dimension. For instance, what about the nurses who are on their lunch breaks? Are they on duty, on call, or off duty? They are probably somewhere in between the first two. How about the nurses sitting at the nurse's station who see the signal light blinking in a patient's room and who get up to find out what the patient wants? Are they operating at the same level of accessibility or attention both before and after they responded to the light? We would have to say no, that they increased their level of accessibility once they entered the patient's room. And so on and so forth, such that we can see that the day-to-day operation of *any* continuous-coverage social system involves a series of coordinated efforts to provide some level of care to someone.

Fire departments, police stations, and military bases are other examples of continuous-coverage social systems that immediately come to mind. But when you think about it, families with infants are continuous-coverage social systems too (LaRossa and LaRossa, 1981). New parents quickly discover that continuous coverage is something that they are expected to provide. Only, unlike in a hospital, patients are not the ones being "covered"; babies are. Thus, the parents of a newborn must care for their child regardless of the time of the day, the day of the week, or the time of the year. They must, in other words, *always* be accessible to their baby. Even if they hire a baby-sitter they are still "on call," as evidenced by the fact that they will leave a phone number where they can be reached. If the baby is sleeping, they might be able to attend temporarily to their own needs—get in some private time—but when the baby signals for help (typically by crying), they or their representative—again the baby-sitter—must respond in much the same way as the nurses who are on duty, but perhaps resting, must respond to the patient whose emergency light is blinking.

Continuous-coverage social systems generally deal with having to be always accessible by establishing a division of labor. For example, in a hospital the day, evening, and night shifts formally divide responsibility for continuous medical coverage—that is, elaborate schedules are devised and staff members sign in and out (Zerubavel, 1979).

Continuous-coverage family systems also set up a division of labor, although seldom in the same way that other coverage systems do. Some of the difference stems from the fact that families are not as formal as hospitals, fire departments, military bases, and the like. Hence, child caregivers typically are not as interchangeable. For instance, we tend to consider the three shifts in a hospital functionally equivalent; as far as we are concerned, the nurses on the night shift can replace the nurses on the evening shift without doing harm to the patients. By contrast, we in America tend to believe that parents—and especially mothers—are irreplaceable. Teachers, baby-sitters, and grandparents can perhaps *substitute* for parents (and do so on a regular basis), but in the opinion of most people in this country they cannot *replace* parents.

One thing about a division of labor is that the coordination it entails tends to make the people involved more dependent on one another (Zerubavel, 1981). Thus, when people have children they become more dependent on their spouses, their relatives, their friends, and the community at large to "cover" for them (that is, care for their children when they cannot). Increased dependency on others generally enhances solidarity and increases social interaction. This is why new parents (1) often feel that they and their spouses have become more like coworkers, sacrificing intimacy in the process (Belsky et al., 1983; LaRossa and LaRossa, 1981), and (2) report spending more time with their parents as well as with friends and acquaintances who have children (Belsky and Rovine, 1984; Fischer, 1981; O'Donnell, 1982).

To sum up what I have said up to now, the nature of infant care is that it involves responsibility for human beings who are unable to fend for themselves and who consequently demand a tremendous amount of people's private time. In order to provide the care that newborns demand, while simultaneously ensuring a modicum of freedom for the caregivers, families with infants will organize themselves into continuous-coverage social systems, varying both the level of attention that their infants receive at any given moment and the personnel responsible for furnishing that attention.

NOT EVERY BABY IS ALIKE

Continuous infant care is complex for a number of reasons, not the least of which is that babies differ so much. Some babies are mature at birth, others are not. Some are healthy, others are physically or mentally handicapped. There is also the fact that babies change—rapidly. Several months can mean the difference between not being able to sit and being able to walk (and "get into things").

Prematurity, Size, and Growth

Babies differ by gestational age, by weight, and by fetal growth rate. Although most babies are born between 38 and 42 weeks of gestation, some are born "early" (that is, prematurely) and some are born "late" (that is, postmaturely). Also, although the average baby born in the United States weighs between 2,900 and 4,100 grams (6 pounds, 5 ounces to 8 pounds, 15 ounces), there are babies who are born a lot smaller or larger. Finally, babies generally grow in utero at a rate that is appropriate for their gestational age, but some babies do grow at a retarded or accelerated rate.

What difference do these distinctions make? Premature babies, low birth-weight babies, and small for gestational age babies generally are more helpless than normal babies and hence require more care.[1]

Take the case of prematurity. Most of the infants who end up in a neonatal intensive care unit after birth are premature infants. These babies, having been born too soon, often have immature respiratory and circulatory systems, among other problems.

In general, respirations in the preterm infant are irregular, rapid, and sometimes shallow, with periods of apnea and cyanosis [i.e., respiratory arrest and oxygen deficiency]. . . . The preterm infant's heart [also] is relatively large at birth compared to his overall body size, and murmurs [i.e., atypical sounds of the heart indicating abnormality] are not uncommon [Miller and Brooten, 1983: 626, 634].

Neonatal intensive care units are a sight to behold. One is "struck by the pace of activity, . . . the sophisticated technology, and the life and death struggle that is a regular part of the routine." And to see tiny babies, some weighing no more than a pound, "attached to respirators, oxygen dispensers, I.V.s [intravenous tubes], . . . with monitors beeping warnings of heart arrest" is a gut-wrenching experience (Bogdan et al., 1982: 7).

The relationship between the helplessness of infants and the continuity of care for infants becomes abundantly clear in these units. The high staff-to-baby ratio, the intensity of concentration of the caregivers, the employment of electronic sensors all lend support to the proposition that *the more helpless the infant, the more continuous the care.* Which is to say that the more helpless the infant, the greater the proportion of on-duty time (total accessibility) and on-call time (ready on a moment's notice) vis-à-vis that infant.

Premature infants may require intensive care for as long as two to four months and, in extremely complicated cases, may be in the hospital for as long as a year. No doubt being premature is a tough way to begin one's life.

Being the father or mother of a premature infant also is a tough way to begin parental life. Not only must you deal with the fact that your transition to parenthood has come weeks or months earlier than you had expected, you also must cope with the physical reality that your baby is very sick and perhaps may die, and the social reality that he or she is not home with you but in a hospital. The nature of parental care is different too. Here is what one study discovered about the kind of attention that the hospital staff expected of these parents:

1. The parents were expected to assume heightened social responsibility by keeping all other aspects of their lives organized so they could direct their attention exclusively to their infants' and staff's needs. Parents had to be available to consent to emergency procedures and share the responsibility of their failure.

2. The parents had to restrain their emotions, both so they could participate intelligently in the decisions that had to be made and leave staff free to concentrate on treatment.

3. The parents were expected to minimize their own sense of responsibility and guilt for their infant's condition.

4. Although the parents realized that the cost of care in the neonatal unit
ran about $750 a day or more . . . they were not supposed to let financial
worries override their concern for their infants.

5. The parents were obligated to seek help from competent specialists,
follow their advice, and share in the responsibility for the outcome even
when this course of action conflicted with the parents' emotional,
cultural, and ethical philosophies [Sosnowitz, 1984: 394].

Obviously parents of premature infants (and other infants in
intensive care units) occupy a very unique social world.

Handicapped Infants

Premature babies, low birth-weight babies, and small for gestational
age babies are more likely to suffer from complications that require
neonatal intensive care. However, by no means do these three
categories exhaust the range of physical problems that can beset a
newborn. An infant can arrive on schedule and be just the right size but
still have special needs because he or she, for example, was born with a
cleft palate or club feet, or is discovered to have spina bifida or Down's
syndrome.

The first two problems are, as doctors say, "correctable." A series of
operations can restructure a baby's palate and casting and/or surgery
can straighten a club foot. But before and during the time these
corrections are being made (which may take months, perhaps years),
the level of parental care that is required is pretty intense. A mother
whose daughter was born with a cleft palate explains:

Most cleft palate children must be fed with a special cleft palate feeder,
bubble syringe, or medicine dropper, but luckily Shari was able to use a
regular bottle fit with a special nipple. Still, she took very little milk at each
feeding, chewing on the nipple rather than actually sucking. When I finally
got her home, feeding would be an all-day affair with one mealtime sliding
into the next because formula was taken so slowly [Hunter, 1982: 125].

Weekly visits to the doctor, periodic operations (and/or castings),
and the simple fact that, despite the long-term benefits, correcting a
cleft palate or club foot physically *hurts* the baby also take their toll on
new parents.

Babies whose disabilities are more severe and more permanent place even a greater strain on their parents. It is not simply that infants with spina bifida or Down's syndrome (or any other congenital defect) require a lot of attention, it's also the emotional anguish that parents must learn to live with.

Following a Lamaze delivery, my husband and I rejoiced over our beautiful baby girl. Consequently, I was stunned the next morning when our family doctor tried to tell me as gently as he could, "Your baby is a mongoloid." I had no idea what he meant, but knew it was not good. In that split second it seemed as though my neatly organized life had been shattered. . . . I discovered feelings in myself I never knew existed. My reaction ranged from bitterness to pity for myself and my child. There was a child in the nursery with a cleft palate, and I would hear people murmuring about how sad it was for the baby and the parents. I couldn't help but think although my baby looked normal to them, her problem wasn't correctable by surgery, as that child's was [Kinman, 1982: 138-139].

Parents of permanently disabled children are likely to experience a host of feelings—fear, anger, loneliness, guilt, and self-doubt are especially common (Featherstone, 1980)—and it is difficult, if not impossible, to fully convey what their world is like. As one father of a child with a fatal disease put it, "The only way a person can know what it is like to be the parent of a handicapped child is to be one" (Klein, 1980: 55).

Infant Temperament

One of the most famous lines in English literature is Leo Tolstoy's opening to his novel, *Anna Karenina* (1878): "Happy families are all alike; every unhappy family is unhappy in its own way." Tolstoy's thesis may be poetical, but it is flat-out wrong. Studies show that happy families are *not* all alike, that happy families differ in their own ways, too.

Up until recently child psychologists subscribed to a view of infants similar to Tolstoy's view of families. They believed that, although enormous differences existed among abnormal infants, normal infants were all essentially alike. On the basis of new research, however, child psychologists now tell us that they were mistaken, that infants do vary considerably. Second, they state that an infant's temperament or

disposition is not simply a product of socialization, but that infants are
different at birth. Third, child psychologists have been able to docu-
ment that *differences in infant temperament have an impact on the
behavior of their caregivers* (Bell and Harper, 1977; Roberts and
Miller, 1978).

How do babies differ from one another? Basically in nine ways:
"activity level, rhythmicity (regularity) of biological functions, approach
or withdrawal to the new, adaptability to new or altered situations,
sensory threshold of responsiveness to stimuli, intensity of reaction,
quality of mood, distractibility, and attention span and persistence"
(Thomas and Chess, 1980: 71). Thus, for example, normal babies can
be very active, irregular when it comes to sleeping, yell and scream
when confronted with new experiences, and hate to change old habits.
They also may have a low tolerance for noise, be in a bad mood no
matter what you do, respond with great intensity and energy to almost
any situation, be unable to concentrate for even short periods of time,
and act extremely stubborn to boot. And other babies may be just
the opposite.

About 10% of all babies are what may be called "difficult" babies
(Thomas and Chess, 1980). In terms of the characteristics specified
above, these babies are the perennial criers, the poor sleepers, the ones
who seem to be impossible to please. The level of care that these babies
demand can place considerable stress on parents.

> Baby cried especially at night. . . . He seemed colicky [i.e., to have pain in
> his stomach]. In spite of medicines he seemed to get worse. Sometimes I
> used to be quite rough in putting the medicine into his mouth. I started
> feeling more and more detached from him. Since my husband was a man
> that couldn't cope with a child crying, I had to shut myself in a room with
> baby and pace the floor with him, for hours. I believe baby could feel lack
> of love from me. He became so much worse that I spent most of the day
> and night walking the floor with him. At times I only had one hour's sleep,
> and during these times I wanted to throw the baby against the wall. These
> feelings were so strong and real, that I found it a little hard to distinguish
> which thought was most real.

This is an excerpt from one of hundreds of letters that child
developmental specialist John Kirkland has received since he founded a
clinic for people whose babies are "criers" (Kirkland, 1983; Kirkland
et al., 1983). The clinic—called CrySOS—helps fathers and mothers to

better understand what makes infants cry and teaches parents how to deal effectively with their crying babies.

You will note that one of the feelings expressed by the mother in the above letter is the urge to throw her baby against the wall. She also admits that sometimes she can be quite rough with the baby when giving him his medicine. Infants who are difficult to care for—not only infants who cry a lot, but also premature and low birth-weight infants as well as physically and mentally handicapped infants—have a greater risk of being abused by their parents or caregivers. Indeed, "any child who is considered somehow 'different' seems to run a slightly greater risk of maltreatment" (Gelles and Cornell, 1985: 54).

The Ever-Changing Infant

Babies change over time and, in the process, place different demands on their caregivers. For example, a two-week-old infant no doubt is helpless, but it also may sleep a lot, and it cannot turn over or crawl. Thus, the parents of a two-week-old will find that while the baby is sleeping or, if it is awake, while it is sitting in its infant seat or lying in its crib, they can do a lot of things that they were able to do before it was born (for example, eat dinner or watch television without being interrupted). In other words, these parents will learn, as other continuous-coverage caregivers have learned, that they need not be completely accessible to fulfill their responsibilities. Being halfway accessible (on call) may be just as effective as being completely accessible (on duty).

But what about when the baby gets older? In some ways the level of coverage increases. Older babies tend to sleep less and they are more mobile, being able to crawl and perhaps walk (toddle). Parents of a 12-month-old child often will complain that they must be more vigilant to ensure that the baby will not hurt itself by climbing out of its crib or poking its finger in an electrical socket. The parents' lives seem more hectic because they must interact more with the baby—that is, be accessible more frequently to their baby—to keep it safe and amused. Some parents attempt to reduce the intensity of their on-duty time by "baby proofing" their home. They may, for example, remove small objects from the coffee table and insert plastic plugs in all the electrical outlets. Most baby-proofing measures, however, are only a stopgap.

Conscientious parents soon learn that they still have to keep an eye on (be accessible to) their children.

PARENTAL COMMITMENT

The level of care that babies receive is not only a function of what they are like (and how helpless they happen to be) but also a function of how committed their parents are to caring for them. And how committed parents are to caring for their babies depends primarily on two things: the parents' theories about children and their affection for their children.

Theories About Children

Two sets of parents might have babies who, besides being born on the same day, are equally healthy and have the same temperament. Yet the level of coverage provided the babies might differ drastically because of the different theories about children that the parents happen to believe in. The first set of parents may believe that it is bad for fathers and mothers to attend to their children whenever the children want them to because the parents then run the risk of spoiling them. On the other hand, the second set of parents may believe that fathers and mothers should attend to their children whenever the children want them to because, if they do not, their children will think that they do not like them. The first set of parents appears to be less protective of their baby than the second, and thus we would expect that the level of coverage in the first family would be lower than that in the second. (For example, the baby falls and starts to cry, but apparently is not hurt. Do you immediately console the child? The first set of parents might say no; the second set, yes.)

Throughout history children have been treated (nurtured, disciplined, raised) in a variety of ways, and the parenting strategies that are used at a particular time appear to be connected to the theories about children that are popular at that time (Skolnick, 1983: 321-348).

During the Middle Ages, for example, three- and four-year-old children were perceived as *miniature adults*. Not only did they dress like adults (that is, in clothes that adults wore, only smaller), they also acted like adults, playing adult games and taking part in adult celebrations (Aries, 1962).

Then there is the image of children as *little demons*. The theory here (advanced by John Calvin among others) is that children basically are corrupt and need harsh discipline if they are to grow to be upstanding citizens. Parents who subscribe to this view often will take the proverb "Spare the rod and spoil the child" literally and whippings and other forms of child abuse are commonly employed.

The Romantic school of writers saw children as *noble savages*. Romanticists believed that a child's perception was more valid than that of an adult because it had not yet been deadened by industrial society. Jean Jacques Rousseau, a leading figure in the Romantic school, once said, for example, "Everything degenerates in the hands of man" (1762). With his emphasis on allowing the natural positive forces in children to develop without restraint, Rousseau is often cited as the father of parental permissiveness (Borstelmann, 1983).

During the Victorian age children were perceived as *innocent beings* and childhood was seen as a time for play. James M. Barrie's *Peter Pan* (1904), about a fantasy land where children never grew up, epitomizes the image of children popular at this time.

The twentieth century—and the works of psychologists such as G. Stanley Hall, Sigmund Freud, and Jean Piaget—ushered in a view of children as *developing beings*. Developmental psychologists believe that beginning at birth the child embarks on a journey that involves a series of maturational steps. Some developmental psychologists also believe that how well the child navigates through the early stages of his or her life will have an effect on what happens later on. A child, for example, who is unable to master the developmental tasks of Stage I will be ill-equipped to deal with the developmental tasks of Stages II, III, IV, and so on.

Although parents today are apt to use parts of all of these theories when raising their children, the theory of children that currently is in vogue—particularly among the most educated in this society—is the theory that children are developing beings (Skolnick, 1983: 325). This paradigm, in fact, is so popular that it has spawned an entire industry— the parent education business.

Every college and university and almost every high school offers courses in child development and developmental psychology, and books and magazines that promise to help parents develop their children's potential are very much in demand.

> Baby books have multiplied like diaper rash; the national Waldenbooks chain carries 250 titles, and sales zoomed 64 percent . . . when they

moved them to the front of the store. Magazines—*Parents, American Baby, Working Mother*—abound, and so do newslettters; *Growing Baby* will send you one specialized bulletin per month of preschool life, up to six years [Langway et al., 1983: 68].

Even the toy industry has tried to cash in on the interest parents have in helping their babies climb the developmental ladder. Johnson and Johnson has begun to market a full line of toys designed to "improve" a "baby's skills." The company's baby rattle, for example, is not sold by itself but with a 17-page "child development publication" that instructs parents how to help their babies "learn while they play."

The superbaby movement also is an outgrowth of the child developmental paradigm. A lot of parents are pushing their infants through rigorous educational programs—trying to make them "super-babies"—because they believe that doing so will ensure their child's future success. One mother of two children (a nine-week-old and a three-year-old) summed up the feeling of many of them when she said,

There's so much pressure to get into college. . . . You have to start them young and push them on toward their goal. They have to be aware of everything—the alphabet, numbers, reading. I want to fill these little sponges as much as possible [Langway et al., 1983: 62].

What is significant about the developmental paradigm is the level of commitment that is expected of the parents. The Johnson and Johnson publications encourage parents not to simply hand the toys to their babies but to *work hard* at getting their babies to use the toys properly. The gurus of the superbaby movement recommend that parents *work hard* at teaching their babies to read, write, and do arithmetic. In other words, according to the developmental paradigm, being a good parent requires more than being "on call" (for example, within earshot) when children are around; being a good parent means being "on duty" whenever possible and devoting that on-duty time to instructional activities.

Of course, not every developmental psychologist is a superbaby advocate (only a small minority are), and not all parents feel compelled to teach their infants how to read or to use a computer immediately. But there is no denying that the developmental paradigm strongly encourages parents to *interact* with their babies—that is, to talk to and cuddle their babies—and, as a result, is responsible for increasing the general level of parental commitment in this society and the overall quality of parent-infant contact.

Affection for Children

Several years ago a soldier stationed at Fort Benning, Georgia, pleaded guilty to charges of cruelty to a child. His five-month-old daughter died of a ruptured blood vessel in the brain, and during the course of the police investigation the following facts surfaced. The child would often be left alone for more than ten hours each day while her father went to work. She had gone without food and water for three days before she died. She had been kept in a trailer without heat. It was December (Atlanta Journal, 1981).

Much of what I have been saying up to now presumes that parents love their children enough to protect them from serious harm. (Even parents who view their babies as little demons and who rely on corporal punishment can still love their children.) However, as the story of the Fort Benning soldier demonstrates, not all parents love their children as much as you and I might love our children.

It may seem strange for me to suggest that the amount of love that some parents have for their children can be less or more than the amount of love that other parents have for their children. After all, don't all parents love their kids? The evidence suggests that the answer is no. Scholars recently have begun to question the age-old idea that parental love is a natural phenomenon, that just because you are biologically tied to your children you necessarily have a great deal of affection for your children.

Historians tell us that during the seventeenth and eighteenth centuries parents "viewed the development and happiness of infants younger than two with indifference" (Shorter, 1975: 168). For example, although we are offended by the idea that a father would leave his daughter alone while he went to work, this practice was common in Europe 250 years ago. Sometimes infants would be left alone in their cradles, other times they would be *swaddled*, which means they would be bandaged from head to foot so they could not move and then hung on a hook or tree limb for hours on end, often stewing in their own excrement. Another practice—especially common in France during the seventeenth and early eighteenth centuries—was that of sending infants away for as long as two to four years to be breastfed by a paid wet nurse.

In Paris in 1780, out of 21,000 children born (in a population of 800,000 to 900,000), fewer than 1,000 were nursed by their mothers, while another 1,000 were nursed by live-in wet nurses. All the others—that would be 19,000—were sent away to wet nurses. Out of these 19,000, only 2,000 to 3,000, whose parents had comfortable incomes, were placed in the nearby suburb of Paris. The other, less fortunate ones were packed off to distant locations [Badinter, 1980: 42-43].

Parents seldom visited the infants they had sent away to be nursed. What little they knew about their babies' growth and development typically they learned by mail.

Dear Madame,

I'm writing to give you news of your precious dear, and at the same time to ask how you yourself are getting along. The little darling is fine. He has just had a touch of rickets [!], but I took him on a pilgrimmage which cost me three francs and now he's doing much better. It's astonishing how much he resembles your husband. Might I ask you to send me booties, for he'll be walking soon. It's also soon going to be time to get him into clothes. His toothing has been so difficult that I've had to put sugar into everything he takes. Would it be convenient for you to send along a bit of sugar and some soap. My regard to your husband.

Your nurse, [Shorter, 1975: 178].

More often than not, the reason behind leaving babies home (in or out of swaddling clothes) or sending them away to wet nurses was financial. For example, "butchers' and bakers' wives traditionally kept the shop. If a mother nursed her child, her husband would be forced to hire someone to take her place. . . . [And economically] it cost less to send a child to a nurse than it did to hire an unskilled laborer" (Badinter, 1980: 48). However, some parents were not financially strapped and yet chose to leave their babies unattended or in the hands of a faraway nurse anyway. How do we account for their behavior?

For a long time scholars have claimed that the high infant mortality rate discouraged parents from becoming attached to their babies. Because an infant's chances of survival were slim (in some parts of Europe in the seventeenth century as many as four out of ten babies died before their first birthday), it was argued that parents avoided the trauma of watching a loved one die by not allowing themselves to develop a fondness for their babies too soon (see, for example, Aries,

1962: 38). Some scholars, however, have begun to turn the issue around, saying that the high infant mortality rate in traditional society was not the cause but the result of an absence of parental affection for babies.

> If children perished in great numbers, it wasn't owing to the intervention of some *deus ex machina* beyond the parents' control [e.g., famine and disease]. It came about as a result of circumstances over which the parents had considerable influence: infant diet, age at weaning, cleanliness of bed linen, and the general hygienic circumstances that surround the child—to say nothing of less tangible factors in mothering, such as picking up the infant, talking and singing to it, giving it the feeling of being loved in a secure little universe [Shorter, 1975: 203-204].

In other words, some parents did not care for their infants *because they did not want to care for their infants.* And why did they not want to care for their infants? Because they were more enamored with their marital, occupational, and leisurely pursuits than they were with their babies (Badinter, 1980).

Social psychologists tell us that our commitment to any activity is, to some degree, a function of the social value of that activity compared to the social value of alternative activities (Thibaut and Kelley, 1959). That is to say, how much you want to do something—how committed you are to doing something—depends on what your other options are. If you have no other options, you basically are forced into a line of action and may very well develop a liking for it, if only to make yourself feel better ("It isn't so bad after all"). On the other hand, if you have a lot of options, you generally will choose the option that has the most value to you.

Some parents in eighteenth-century France simply felt they had "better" things to do than care for their babies.

> Children interfered not only with the mother's conjugal life but also with her amusements. To busy oneself with a child was neither enjoyable nor chic. . . . The pleasures of the woman of the world were to be found principally in social life: receiving guests and paying visits, showing off a new dress, running to the opera and theater [Badinter, 1980: 70-71].

What about now; are there any parents today who dislike their children as much as some parents in eighteenth-century Europe apparently disliked their children? Well, first of all, the Fort Benning incident is not an isolated case. There are thousands of children each year who are neglected by their parents—children who are left alone when their parents go to work or to a movie, children who are ignored because their parents feel they have "better" things to do than care for their kids (Gelles and Cornell, 1985).

Some sociologists feel that, indeed, although affection for children rose during the nineteenth and twentieth centuries, in the past twenty years or so it has declined somewhat (Badinter, 1980: 327-328). And one sociologist has gone so far as to say that modern Western society "is profoundly hostile to children," that basically adults today "do not like children" (Greer, 1984: 2).

I think it is extreme to say that *all* of Western society is indifferent to children (just the same as it would be extreme to say that all of eighteenth-century Europe was indifferent to children), but I do think that over the past 20 years some segments of our society increasingly have come to view children as nuisances. I am not talking about couples who decide to remain childfree. I am talking about *parents* who see their own kids as intrusions.

If, again, it is correct that your commitment to an activity is a function of that activity's relative social value, then we cannot overlook the fact that, as our society has become more career-oriented (that is, more people than before live to work rather than work to live) and more leisure-oriented, child care has, for some, become less "attractive" (LaRossa, 1983).

For example, there is the newspaper story about a San Francisco father who was jogging around Golden Gate Park and who apparently was so caught up in running that he failed to notice his three-year-old daughter—whom he had brought with him—crying, "Daddy, Daddy" along the side of the track. On his next trip around, he finally heard her, but stopped only long enough to tell her that he would not be watching for her, *she should be watching for him* (Gustatis, 1982)—an interesting twist on the problem of continuous coverage. The reporter who wrote the piece wondered how many other parents today are so caught up in their own pursuits that they cannot find time for their crying children. My guess is that there probably are a lot more than we realize.

You might ask, why do some people become parents if they cannot be bothered with their kids? I would simply remind you that the decision to become a parent is made under a lot of pronatalistic pressure (society views people who become parents as "normal" and those who do not as "selfish," "weird," and so on); and that parenthood being what it is, there are many people who do not really know how they feel about children *until* they have their own (unlike other jobs, you cannot practice being a father or mother). In other words, there are social-structural conditions that make it inevitable that people who are uncommitted to child care will end up having children.

There is another reason it is wrong to say that *all* of Western society is indifferent to children. Such a general condemnation overlooks the fact that many, if not most, parents today are extremely fond of their children. Indeed, although everything I have said about caring for infants is true—continuous coverage does demand a lot of attention—parents generally are willing to put up with the dirty diapers and the sleepless nights because *they love their children dearly.*

It is hard to communicate the emotional attachment that parents develop for their children. If you are a parent yourself, you probably need no explanation. It is not a sexual love, but it is a physical love. Holding your baby close to you can bring out goosebumps, and tears are not uncommon. During the seventeenth and eighteenth centuries many parents did not grieve at the death of an infant (Badinter, 1980; Shorter, 1975). Nowadays, a baby's death is a heart-wrenching experience, one from which some parents never recover (Peppers and Knapp, 1980). Parental love also is not limited to mothers. There are many fathers today who go "ga-ga" over their kids. In a study of men who share child-care responsibilities with their wives, a father confessed that he was "absolutely in love . . . passionately in love" with his daughter (Ehrensaft, 1985).

If you can remember, I said early on that becoming a parent is fraught with contradictions, that it takes a tremendous amount of effort, but that it is also one of the most rewarding experiences that a person can have. The interesting thing about the contradictions, however, is that the negative aspects of becoming a parent typically have to do with what sociologists call the *instrumental* side of a relationship (for example, the increased amount of work) whereas the positive aspects often are on the *expressive* side (someone to love). The fact that we know more about the negative than we do the positive—there is a lot more transition to parenthood research on the former than on the latter—may be due to the tendency of social scientists to focus on the instrumental rather than the expressive. My hope is that the recent interest in the "sociology of emotions" (Kemper, 1981) will motivate scholars to begin to examine more carefully the expressive side of the parent-infant relationship.

In sum, affection for children is not a natural phenomenon that remains constant and is the same for all parents; rather, it is a social process that changes over time and is different for different people. How much parents like or love their children is related to how much they are committed to caring for their children: Generally speaking, *the greater the love, the greater the commitment.*

FATHERS VERSUS MOTHERS

Quantitative and Qualitative Differences

Much attention has been devoted lately to what has been called the "new father." Stereotypically speaking, the new father does not want to make the mistake that he believes his father did; he does not want to be so absorbed with his job and friends that he neglects his children. So the new father makes the effort to spend more time with his kids, to be the dad he never had. The new father also does not wait until his children are older before he gets to know them; he starts early. He enjoys feeling the baby kick inside his wife's tummy. He demands to be present at the birth to greet the new arrival and take the first pictures. And, as much as he might not like it, he throws himself into the responsibilities of continuous infant care, changing the dirtiest diapers and accepting his share of the midnight-to-six feedings.

How real is the new father? He is real enough, but he is nowhere near as prevalent as some would have us believe. Fathers today indeed are involved with their children more than their own fathers were with them, but they still lag far behind mothers. Study after study after study shows that when it comes to child care women still bear the major brunt of the responsibility.

Fathers of preschool children (youngest child 0 to 5 years old), for example, spend about a half-hour a day in child-care activities, whereas mothers of preschool children spend close to two hours a day in these activities. You may argue that this is an unfair comparison because (according to the U.S. Bureau of Labor Statistics, 1981) one-half of the mothers of preschool children are not employed, giving them more opportunities to be with their kids (see also Waite et al., 1985). But even if we control for employment and examine only families in which both the husband and wife work outside the home, significant differences still exist. Fathers whose wives are employed do *not* interact with their children any more than fathers whose wives are unemployed; both spend, again, about a half-hour a day in child-care activities. As for mothers, those who are unemployed spend a little over two hours a day interacting with their children, and those who are employed spend about an hour and a half a day (Pleck, 1983).

Studies that have examined the division of infant care, per se, generally report the same unbalanced picture. In one sample of couples, for example, fathers contributed only 13% of the total needed care when their babies were three weeks old and no more than 17% when their babies were three months old (Katsh, 1981). Again, you may argue that the fathers probably are not at home as much as are the mothers (who may be on maternity leave). But even in dual-earner families, fathers spend significantly less time with their babies than do mothers (LaRossa and LaRossa, 1981).

The amount of time that fathers and mothers spend with their children is not the only distinction between fathering and mothering, nor is it necessarily the most important. Research indicates that the time that fathers spend with their infants often comes under the heading of "play," whereas the time that mothers spend with their infants typically involves "custodial activities," such as diaper changing, feeding, and bathing (Katsh, 1981). As for the kind of play that fathers engage in with their infants, generally speaking, "father-infant play shift[s] rapidly from peaks of high infant attention and excitement to valleys of minimal attention, while mother-infant play demonstrate[s] more gradual shifts" (Parke, 1981). In other words, the little time that fathers spend with their infants is likely to be broken up into short segments.

Fathers also are not likely to spend much time alone with their babies, which means that their perception of what it means to be ever accessible to a newborn is somewhat distorted. They may think they know what infant care is all about, priding themselves on how much they do at night or on the weekend, but what they often fail to realize is how much easier it is to care for a baby when there are two adults around.

One father, a physics professor who had never spent any time alone with his infant son, told his wife that he was disappointed over her lack of activity. *Why*, he asked, had she stopped sewing? *When*, she responded, does she have the time, given that she was home with the baby all day? The father could not understand how taking care of a one-month-old baby would prevent someone from sewing, so his wife challenged him to spend one day *by himself* with his son. The father accepted the challenge, and here (in abbreviated form) is how the day went:

8:45 Got up from bed to shower. Edward quiet.

8:55 In shower. Edward crying. Got out of shower.

9:10 Edward quiet again. Why? Who knows. Back to shower.

10:00 Blessed! Edward sleeping, me showered and shaved and dressed. Elapsed time for shower & dress: one hour fifteen minutes.

10:30 Bed made/dishes done. Amazingly easy. Sit down to read [physics] report.

11:00 Report difficult—fifteen pages read when Edward awakens.

11-11:30 Ellen has marked down this hour for play. How do you play with Edward? Too young to bounce. Put . . . on stereo and waltzed him. Hard to know what he makes of it. He stares at speakers.

11:45 Mystery solved. Edward needed bowel movement; hence, the concentrated stare. Bowel movement fouls

(a) his diaper and stretchy suit

(b) my shirt sleeve

(c) living-room carpet.

12:15 Diaper, suit, and my shirt changed. Carpet scrubbed. Edward wailing for bottle. Very healthy cry, which I rarely hear. Does he miss mommy? The rat!

12:40 Edward fed and sleeping. Me reading.

1:55 I wake up. I do not know when I fell asleep or why. Checking watch, it appears I have about thirty-forty minutes before the baby gets up and needs food again. I need food, too.

2:15 Half-grilled cheese sandwich comes out of oven prematurely when Edward cries. Cheese still cold in middle. Eaten in four gulps as Edward becomes desperate. Milk (for me, already poured) will have to wait.

2:55 Edward is inconsolable. I *can't* feed him again yet. First of all, the remaining milk is frozen. Secondly, it isn't time yet. What to do?

3:05 Defrosting milk in pan of water. Edward wailing. Blood pressure going through roof. Every minute counts. Ellen gets back at three-thirty. Can I make it? [Jaffe and Viertel, 1979: 130-131].

In the end, Ellen returned home at 3:45—fifteen minutes late—and was met by a "snarling husband": "Goddamit," he said as she walked in the door, "don't you ever be late again, not for anything!"

Fathers also are rarely involved in the psychic division of labor in parenting (Ehrensaft, 1983). I am talking about keeping in one's head the knowledge of when it is time to take the baby to the doctor, or when it is time to shift from strained to solid foods, or when it is time to buy new clothes, and so on. (Note, for instance, that the physics professor says that his wife *told him* when it was time to play with his son.)

The willingness of fathers to relegate these psychic tasks to their wives and the willingness of mothers to take responsibility for the tasks in the first place underscores the fact that fathers generally are perceived as surrogate parents or mothers' helpers. It is interesting, in this regard, to note how often fathers will refer to their time spent with their children as "baby-sitting," which is something that mothers seldom do when referring to their own parenting activities (LaRossa and LaRossa, 1981). To *baby-sit* is "to care for children usually during a short absence of parents" (Webster's New Collegiate Dictionary, 1977: 81). Technically speaking, fathers cannot baby-sit for their own children because they are the parents of their children. The fact, however, that men see themselves as baby-sitters says a lot about how they see themselves as fathers. Apparently, to many men being a father means residing on the periphery of parenthood.

Even when fathers try to go beyond being mothers' helpers, when they try to *share* child care (for example, by regularly alternating child care with their wives), they still come up short in that their identities (their sense of who they are) are rarely as closely tied to fatherhood as their wives' identities are to motherhood (Ehrensaft, 1985). Another way of phrasing it is that in contrast to mothers "the sharing father more likely enters the parenting experience with a notion that parenting is something you *do* rather than someone you are" (Ehrensaft, 1983: 55).

Explaining the Differences

Explaining why the division of infant care is so unbalanced—recent changes notwithstanding—is one of the thorniest issues in the behavioral and social sciences. It is also one of the most important.

Some people believe that the differences are purely a function of biology, that there exists a "maternal instinct" that programs women to not only *want* to nurture their young but also *know how* to nurture their young. More often than not, those who subscribe to this view draw parallels between nonhumans and humans.

It is true that some nonhuman primates exhibit child-care patterns similar to those of humans; but one should not overlook the fact that the parallels are far from perfect. Male rhesus monkeys, for example, often exhibit little interest in infants, but they also are known to "groom" infants to the same extent as female rhesus monkeys do, and their interactions with their young are "enhanced" when females are not present (Redican, 1976). Evidence showing that there have been periods in history when the level of maternal infant care has been anything but high (for example, evidence of maternal indifference during the seventeenth and eighteenth centuries) also suggests that an instinctual explanation is incomplete (Badinter, 1980).

A second explanation for the unbalanced division of infant care is Alice Rossi's "biosocial" explanation (Rossi, 1977, 1984)—which, you may recall, I discussed in Chapter 1. According to Rossi, chromosomal, hormonal, and neural differences between men and women account for differences in fathering and mothering. For instance, she argues that because of their biological makeup (for example, their apparent sensitivity to emotional nuance) "women have a head start in easier reading of an infant's facial expressions," and that consequently they are better able to communicate with their young (Rossi, 1984: 13).

Rossi's theory is controversial and has been the subject of debate on several occasions (see Altman et al., 1984; Gross et al., 1979). Some scholars question what they see as Rossi's selective use of the evidence, her tendency to focus only on research that supports her view. Others believe that the biological differences she alludes to are neither consistent nor significant enough to explain fairly large and complex social differences. Gross (1984) points out, for example, that "Rossi's contention that men are less responsive to infants than are women" ignores the research that has shown that "sex [male versus female] differences in responses to infants vary" depending on the situation, the kind of response required, and the subjects' role relationship (for example, stranger, parent) with the child (see Berman, 1980).

I happen to be one of those who believe that Rossi gives too little attention to the part that power and economics play in the division of infant care. I also happen to think, however, that the jury is still out on Rossi's theory and that the next twenty years of research will give us a better idea of how valid the biosocial perspective is. At the very least Rossi has challenged sociologists to examine seriously the relationship between biology and sociology, and that I think is good.

A third explanation for why mothers are more likely than fathers to nurture their children is Nancy Chodorow's "psychoanalytic" explanation (Chodorow, 1978). Building on the work of Sigmund Freud and his followers, Chodorow argues that women have a greater capacity than men to nurture (not only children but other people in general) because the early relationship that women had with their primary caregivers was less problematic than the relationship that men had with theirs. The key, according to Chodorow, is that women generally are raised by members of the *same* gender whereas men are raised by members of the *opposite* gender; that is, both women and men generally are raised by women (mothers), whose own gender parallels that of their daughters but conflicts with that of their sons.

Why would the gender of one's primary caregiver make any difference in one's capacity to nurture?

> Because they are the same gender as their daughters and have been girls, mothers of daughters tend not to experience these infant daughters as separate from them in the same way as do mothers of infant sons. In both cases, a mother is likely to experience a sense of oneness and continuity with her infant. However, this sense is stronger and lasts longer vis-a-vis daughters. . . . Because they are of different gender than their sons, by contrast, mothers experience their sons as a male opposite. Sons tend to be experienced as differentiated from their mothers, and mothers push this differentiation. . . . Girls emerge from this period with a basis for "empathy" built into their primary definition of self in a way that boys do not. Girls emerge with a stronger basis for experiencing another's needs or feelings as one's own (or of thinking that one is so experiencing another's needs and feelings). . . . Masculine personality [by contrast] comes to be defined more in terms of denial of relation and connection [Chodorow, 1978: 109, 110, 167, 169].

Chodorow's theory, like Rossi's, has received considerable attention and has been the subject of debate on more than one occasion (see Lorber et al., 1981; Thurman, 1982). The value of the theory is that it provides an interpretation for the personality differences between men and women that researchers have observed; for example, there is evidence to suggest that women tend to be more empathetic (Rossi, 1981). Also, the theory may constitute at least a partial explanation for why mothers prefer to stay home with their three-month-old infants rather than be employed full time (see Hock et al., 1984). The drawback of the theory, on the other hand, is that it is "culture and time bound."

The problem is that Chodorow is trying to explain the perpetuation of a *certain kind of mothering*—middle class, psychologically oriented, and achievement oriented (husbands and sons toward careers, mothers and daughters toward perfect children)—in short, the hothouse tending of two or three offspring in an isolated nuclear family [Lorber, 1981: 485; italics added].

Simply stated, Chodorow may be guilty of neglecting (or at least unduly minimizing) the extent to which the institution of parenthood is a historical reality.

Which brings me to a fourth explanation for the unequal division of infant care—the "feminist" explanation. This perspective, like the psychoanalytic perspective, sees the relationship that men and women have with their own parents as highly significant, but it is not the sexual anatomy of the child and parent that is considered to be relevant but the child-socialization process itself (for example, the fact that young girls are more likely to be encouraged to perceive parenting as their principal occupation). Another important distinction between the psychoanalytic and feminist perspectives is that the feminist perspective does not focus exclusively on the early years. Feminists believe that socialization during adulthood as well as childhood exerts an influence on people's lives (thus the fact that women of all ages are encouraged to perceive parenting as their principal occupation is of no small importance).

Saying that mothers are more likely to care for babies because they are encouraged to care for babies still leaves unanswered the question, why. *Why* are mothers encouraged to shoulder the responsibility for infant care? The answer that feminists generally offer (in one form or another) is that men are the ones primarily responsible for encouraging women to care for babies because men do not want to care for babies themselves. And why is it that men do not want to care for babies? Because caring for babies "cuts into" their time for doing "more important" things, like making money or moving up the corporate ladder (Polatnick, 1973).

The cornerstone of the feminist explanation is *power*. It is assumed that women have to be convinced to take care of children and that men have the power to do the convincing. Some scholars, however, feel that people cannot be forced to provide the kind of care that infants require and that the feminist explanation, therefore, is inadequate.

> The use of coercion is not possible in the case of mothering. Clinical research shows that behavioral conformity to the apparent specific physical requirements of infants—keeping them fed and clean—is not enough to enable physiological, let alone psychological, growth in an infant. Studies of infants in understaffed institutions where perfunctory care is given, and of infants whose caretakers do not hold them or interact with them, show that these infants may become mildly depressed, generally withdrawn, psychotically unable to relate, totally apathetic and, in extreme cases, may die. . . . Whether or not men in particular or society at large . . . enforce women's mothering, and expect or require a woman to care for her child, they cannot require or force her to provide adequate parenting unless she, *to some degree* and *on some unconscious or conscious level*, has the capacity and sense of self as maternal to do so [Chodorow, 1978: 32-33].

There is something to the idea that parents cannot be coerced to care for their children, but coercion is not the only kind of power there is. People also can be convinced (powered) to do something if they believe that whoever is doing the convincing has the authority (institutionalized right) to control them (Weber, 1947). Thus, for example, people in the United States believe that elected officials have the authority to raise taxes, wage war, and pass laws (or not pass laws—for example, the Equal Rights Amendment).

Feminists also point to the power that men have to construct "ideologies" that make it seem that child care is the "proper" thing for women to do. Hence, feminists are suspicious of cultural ideas such as "mothering is instinctual" because they feel that these ideas can be used to justify keeping women at home with their children.

Finally, feminists argue that men have the power to structure the reward system in a society so that motherhood becomes the best *available* option for women. If you remember, I said earlier that your commitment to an activity is a function of the social value of that activity compared to the social value of alternative activities. If women's alternatives to child care are reduced in value (for example, by putting a ceiling on their job opportunities), then child care may become their most attractive option and the reason behind their high parental commitment. (The flip side of the coin is that men's alternatives to child care are more attractive than child care itself, and that this explains their relatively low parental commitment.)

Where do men get the power to control women's lives? Well, *today* they get it in part from the fact that women are the ones to rear children, which effectively reduces women's economic and political opportunities, making them dependent on men. (The emphasis is on "today" because power relations between men and women vary according to historical circumstances. The reason that childbearing nowadays keeps women out of the labor force is because of the physical separation between work and home brought about by industrialization.) Thus, feminists contend that women's powerlessness derives from their role as child rearers, and their role as child rearers derives from their powerlessness (Polatnick, 1973; see also Trebilcot, 1983).

As you may have already guessed, I am partial to the feminist explanation (see LaRossa, 1977; LaRossa and LaRossa, 1981). I cannot help but be impressed with its sociological underpinnings (that is, the weight that it gives to socialization, power, institutionalization, and so on). On the other hand, I believe that we still have a lot to learn about parenting, and thus would not be surprised if it soon became apparent that only by combining all four explanations (and perhaps others as well) will we ever come to understand the social reality of infant care.

CONCLUSION

"I want to be alone." How many people recognize this statement attributed to Greta Garbo, the actress? Probably quite a few. Interestingly enough, Greta Garbo, herself, claims that her famous remark has always been misquoted, that what she really said was, "I want to be *let* alone" (Bartlett, 1968: 1056). Wanting to be "alone" is a request for private space—a room or house in which you, and only you, reside. Wanting to be "let alone" is a request for *private time*—seconds, minutes, hours, or days that you can be inaccessible to others. One can be in a crowded room and still be let alone. Apparently what Garbo wanted was to be inaccessible.

Becoming a parent has an impact more on one's private time than on one's private space. Sure, you may lose a room to the nursery and your home may not seem as big as it once was, but what really makes a difference in your life once you have a child is the responsibility of having to care for—and be accessible to—someone who needs you. It is this more than anything else that restructures the social world of new parents; and it is this more than anything else that makes parenthood one of our most important social institutions.

I sometimes am asked whether my being a sociologist of parenthood affects what I do as a parent. The answer I always give is "yes." I am a better father than I would have been, had I not come in contact with the sociological perspective. Knowing that my behavior is not fixed, that it is influenced by society, has given me the freedom to choose how I want to live and how I want to relate to my children.

My hope is that by reading this book you also will gain a better understanding of how society shapes you and how you—in concert with others—shape society, and that you will use this fundamental insight to improve your life and that of those around you.

REVIEW QUESTIONS

(1) What does it mean to say that families with infants are "continuous-coverage social systems"?

(2) How do babies differ from one another? What effect do these differences have on new parents?

(3) What are the factors determining how committed parents are to care for their babies?

(4) Who is more likely to be a baby's primary parent—the father or the mother? Why?

SUGGESTED ASSIGNMENTS

(1) Interview a father and mother one month after their child is born. Interview them again several months later. Try to determine if they experience any changes in their attitudes toward their babies, themselves, and their parents. Ask them also how they divide the responsibility for infant care, and whether this changed at all as time went on.

(2) Purchase or borrow the latest edition of Benjamin Spock's book, *Baby and Child Care,* and see if you can detect what Spock's theories about children are and how he feels about maternal and paternal commitment.

(3) Volunteer to baby-sit for someone's infant son or daughter. As you are caring for the child, think about your actions and attitudes (for

example, monitor your on-duty and on-call time and ask yourself how your feelings for the child affect the level of care you provide).

(4) Go someplace where people are likely to take their babies (for example, a playground or shopping mall) and observe how parents interact with their infants and with other parents when in public.

NOTE

1. "Premature babies," "low birth-weight babies," and "small for gestational age babies," are medical terms. Any baby born before 38 weeks is *premature*, regardless of how healthy or large the baby is. Any baby weighing less than 2,500 grams (5 pounds, 7 ounces) is placed in a *low birth-weight* category. Any newborn whose rate of intrauterine growth is below the tenth percentile is considered *small for gestational age* (Gasser, 1981: 143-144).

References

ABRAMS, P. (1982) Historical Sociology. Ithaca, NY: Cornell University Press.

ALTMAN, J., A. K. DANIELS, H. E. GROSS, M. McCLINTOCK, A. ROSSI, and N. SCHWARTZ (1984) "A review panel of Alice S. Rossi's American Sociological Association 1983 presidential address: 'Gender and parenthood.'" Sponsored by Chicago Women in Research and Chicago Sociologists for Women in Society. Panel discussion, University of Illinois at Chicago, January 14.

American Baby: For Expectant and New Parents (1979) Special issue about fathers. Vol. 41 (June). Sponsored by the American Association for Maternal and Child Health.

ANONYMOUS (1820) Remarks on the Employment of Females as Practitioners in Midwifery. Boston.

ANONYMOUS, MD (1972) Confessions of a Gynecologist. Garden City, NY: Doubleday.

ARIES, P. (1962) Centuries of Childhood: A Social History of Family Life. New York: Knopf.

Atlanta Journal (1981) "Soldier admits guilt in death of infant." December 16: 4C.

BACHOFEN, J. J. (1967) Myth, Religion, and Mother Right. Princeton, NJ: Princeton University Press.

BADINTER, E. (1980) Mother Love: Myth and Reality. New York: Macmillan.

BAKER, C. (1977) Am I Parent Material? Washington, DC: National Alliance for Optional Parenthood.

BARASH, D. P. (1977) Sociobiology and Behavior. New York: Elsevier.

BARRIE, J. M. (1904) Peter Pan: Or the Boy Who Would Not Grow Up. New York: Avon.

BARTLETT, J. (1968) Familiar Quotations (E. M. Beck, ed.). Boston: Little, Brown.

BECK, M. with D. WEATHERS, J. McCORMICK, D. T. FRIENDLY, P. ABRAMSON, and M. BRUNO (1985) "America's abortion dilemma." Newsweek (January 14): 20-25.

BECKMAN, L. J. (1982) "Measuring the process of fertility decision-making," pp. 73-95 in G. L. Fox (ed.) The Childbearing Decision: Fertility Attitudes and Behavior. Beverly Hills, CA: Sage.

BEHRMAN, D. L. (1982) Family and/or Career: Plans of First-Time Mothers. Ann Arbor, MI: UMI Research Press.

BELL, R. Q. and L. V. HARPER (1977) Child Effects on Adults. Hillsdale, NJ: Erlbaum.

BELSKY, J. and M. ROVINE (1984) "Social-network contact, family support, and the transition to parenthood." Journal of Marriage and the Family 46 (May): 455-462.

BELSKY, J., G. B. SPANIER, and M. ROVINE (1983) "Stability and change in marriage across the transition to parenthood." Journal of Marriage and the Family 45 (August): 567-577.

BERGER, P. L. and B. BERGER (1972) Sociology: A Biographical Approach. New York: Basic Books.

BERGER, P. L. and T. LUCKMANN (1966) The Social Construction of Reality: A Treatise in the Sociology of Knowledge. Garden City, NY: Doubleday/Anchor.

BERMAN, P. W. (1980) "Are women more responsive than men to the young? a review of developmental and situational variables." Psychological Bulletin 88 (November): 668-695.

BIRCH, W. G. (1982) A Doctor Discusses Pregnancy. Chicago: Budlong Press.

BLUMER, H. (1939) An Appraisal of Thomas and Znaniecki's "The Polish Peasant in Europe and America." New York: Social Science Research Council.

BOGDAN, R., M. A. BROWN, and S. B. FOSTER (1982) "Be honest but not cruel: staff/parent communication on a neonatal unit." Human Organization 41 (Spring): 6-16.

BOMBARDIERI, M. (1981) The Baby Decision: How to Make the Most Important Choice of Your Life. New York: Rawson Associates.

BORSTELMANN, L. J. (1983) "Children before psychology: ideas about children from antiquity to the late 1800s," pp. 1-40 in P. H. Mussen (ed.) Handbook of Child Psychology, Vol. I: History, Theory, and Methods. New York: John Wiley.

Boston Women's Health Book Collective (1978) Ourselves and Our Children: A Book By and For Parents. New York: Random House.

BREEN, D. (1975) The Birth of a First Child: Toward an Understanding of Femininity. London: Tavistock.

BRODERICK, C. E. (1975) "Foreword," in L. Gross (ed.) Sexual Issues in Marriage. New York: Spectrum.

BURCHELL, R. C. (1981) "Cesarean section," pp. 1533-1562 in L. Iffy and H. A. Kaminetzky (eds.) Principles and Practices of Obstetrics and Perinatology, Vol. 2. New York: John Wiley.

CALHOUN, L. G., J. W. SELBY, and H. E. KING (1981) "The influence of pregnancy on sexuality: a review of current evidence." Journal of Sex Research 17 (May): 139-151.

CHERLIN, A. J. (1981) Marriage, Divorce, Remarriage. Cambridge, MA: Harvard University Press.

CHODOROW, N. (1978) The Reproduction of Mothering: Psychoanalysis and the Sociology of Gender. Berkeley: University of California Press.

———(1981) "On The Reproduction of Mothering: a methodological debate." Signs: Journal of Women in Culture and Society 6 (Spring): 500-514.

CHRISTENSEN, H. T. (1968) "Children in the family: relationship of number and spacing marital success." Journal of Marriage and the Family 30 (May): 283-289.

DALLY, A. (1982) Inventing Motherhood: The Consequences of an Ideal. New York: Schocken.

DARLING, R. B. (1979) Families Against Society: A Study of Reactions to Children with Birth Defects. Beverly Hills, CA: Sage.

DAVID, H. P. (1981) "Abortion policies," pp. 1-40 in J. E. Hodgson (ed.) Abortion and Sterilization: Medical and Social Aspects. London: Academic Press.

DEMOS, J. (1970) A Little Commonwealth: Family Life in the Plymouth Colony. New York: Oxford University Press.

DICK-READ, G. (1944) Childbirth Without Fear: The Principles and Practice of Natural Childbirth. New York: Harper & Row.

DINER, H. (1981) "The couvade," pp. 86-90 in D. Meltzer (ed.) Birth: An Anthology of Ancient Texts, Songs, Prayers, and Stories. San Francisco: North Point Press.

ECCLES, A. (1982) Obstetrics and Gynecology in Tudor and Stuart England. Kent, OH: Kent State University Press.

EHRENSAFT, D. (1983) "When women and men mother," pp. 41-61 in J. Trebilcot (ed.) Mothering: Essays in Feminist Theory. Totowa, NJ: Rowan & Allanheld.

———(1985) "Dual parenting and the duel of intimacy," pp. 323-327 in G. Handel (ed.) The Psychosocial Interior of the Family. Hawthorne, NY: Aldine.

ENTWISLE, D. R. and S. G. DOERING (1981) The First Birth: A Family Turning Point. Baltimore: Johns Hopkins University Press.

ESHLEMAN, J. R. and B. G. CASHION (1985) Sociology: An Introduction. Boston: Little, Brown.

FEATHERSTONE, H. (1980) A Difference in the Family: Living with a Disabled Child. New York: Basic Books.

FELDMAN, G. B. and J. A. FREIMAN (1985) "Prophylactic cesarean section at term?" New England Journal of Medicine 312 (May 9): 1264-1267.

FINDLAY, S. (1985) "At-home births: no extra risks." USA Today (March 15): ID.

FISCHER, L. R. (1981) "Transitions in the mother-daughter relationship." Journal of Marriage and the Family 43 (August): 613-622.

FORREST, D. and S. K. HENSHAW (1983) "What U.S. women think and do about contraception." Family Planning Perspectives 15 (August): 157-166.

FOX, V. C. and M. H. QUITT (1980) Loving, Parenting, and Dying. New York: Psychohistory Press.

GASSER, R. F. (1981) "Embryology and fetology," pp. 127-180 in L. Iffy and H. A. Kaminetzky (eds.) Principles and Practice of Obstetrics and Perinatology, Vol. I. New York: John Wiley.

GELLES, R. J. (1975) "Violence and pregnancy: a note of the extent of the problem and needed services." Family Coordinator 24 (January): 81-86.

———and C. P. CORNELL (1985) Intimate Violence in Families. Beverly Hills, CA: Sage.

GILES-SIMS, J. (1983) Wife Battering: A Systems Theory Approach. New York: Guilford Press.

GLADIEUX, J. D. (1978) "Pregnancy—the transition to parenthood," pp. 275-295 in W. B. Miller and L. F. Newman (eds.) The First Child and Family Formation. Chapel Hill: University of North Carolina Press.

GOODE, W. J. (1971) "Force and violence in the family." Journal of Marriage and the Family 33 (November): 624-636.

GOSHEN-GOTTSTEIN, E. R. (1966) Marriage and First Pregnancy: Cultural Influences on Attitudes of Israeli Women. London: Tavistock.

GRAHAM, H. (1976) "The social image of pregnancy: pregnancy as spirit possession." Sociological Review 24 (May): 291-308.

GREER, G. (1984) Sex and Destiny: The Politics of Human Fertility. New York: Harper & Row.

GROSS, H. E. (1984) "Response to Alice Rossi's 'Gender and Parenting.'" Sponsored by Chicago Women in Research and Chicago Sociologists for Women in Society. Panel presentation held at the University of Illinois at Chicago, January 14.

————J. BERNARD, A. J. DAN, N. GLAZER, J. LORBER, M. McCLINTOCK, N. NEWTON, and A. ROSSI (1979) "Considering 'a biosocial perspective on parenting." Signs 4 (Summer): 695-717.

GROSSMAN, F. K., L. S. EICHLER, and S. A. WINICKOFF (1980) Pregnancy, Birth, and Parenthood. San Francisco: Jossey-Bass.

GUSTATIS, R. (1982) "Children sit idle while parents pursue leisure." Atlanta Journal and Constitution (August 15): 1D, 4D.

HANFORD, J. M. (1968) "Pregnancy as a state of conflict." Psychological Reports 22 (June): 1313-1342.

HARRIMAN, L. C. (1983) "Personal and marital changes accompanying parenthood." Family Relations 32 (July): 387-394.

HAWKE, S. and D. KNOX (1977) One Child By Choice. Englewood Cliffs, NJ: Prentice-Hall.

HENSHAW, S. K. and K. O'REILLY (1983) "Characteristics of abortion patients in the United States, 1979 and 1980." Family Planning Perspectives 15 (January/February): 5-16.

HENSLIN, J. (1985) Marriage and Family in a Changing Society. New York: Free Press.

HIMES, N. E. (1970) Medical History of Contraception. New York: Schocken.

HINDS, M. W., G. H. BERGEISEN, and D. T. ALLEN (1985) "Neonatal outcome in planned vs. unplanned out-of-hospital births in Kentucky." Journal of the American Medical Association 235 (March 15): 1578-1582.

HOBBS, D. F. (1965) "Parenthood as crisis: a third study." Journal of Marriage and the Family 27 (August): 367-372.

HOBBS, D. F., Jr. and J. M. WIMBISH (1977) "Transition to parenthood by black couples." Journal of Marriage and the Family 39 (November): 677-689.

HOCK, E., M. T. GNEZDA, and S. L. McBRIDE (1984) "Mothers of infants: attitudes toward employment and motherhood following the birth of the first child." Journal of Marriage and the Family 46 (May): 425-431.

HODGSON, J. E. and R. WARD (1981) "The provision and organization of abortion and sterilization services in the United States," pp. 519-541 in J. E. Hodgson (ed.) Abortion and Sterilization: Medical and Social Aspects. London: Academic Press.

HOFFMAN, L. W. and J. D. MANIS (1978) "Influences of children on marital interaction and parental satisfactions and dissatisfactions," pp. 165-214 in R. M. Lerner and G. B. Spanier (eds.) Child Influences on Marital and Family Interaction: A Life-Span Perspective. New York: Academic Press.

HUANG, L. J. (1982) "Planned fertility of one-couple/one-child policy in the People's Republic of China." Journal of Marriage and the Family 44 (August): 775-784.

HUNTER, C. L. (1982) "Born with a cleft palate," pp. 123-127 in P. Evans (ed.) How a Baby Changed My Life. Wauwatosa, WI: American Baby Books.

JAFFE, S. S. and J. VIERTEL (1979) Becoming Parents: Preparing for the Emotional Changes of First-Time Parenthood. New York: Atheneum.

KATSH, B. S. (1981) "Fathers and infants: reported caregiving and interaction." Journal of Family Issues 2 (September): 275-296.

KAY, M. A. (1982) "Writing an ethnography of birth," pp. 1-24 in M. A. Kay (ed.) Anthropology of Human Birth. Philadelphia: F. A. Davis.

KEMPER, T. D. (1981) "Social constructionist and positivist approaches to the sociology of emotions." American Journal of Sociology 87 (September): 336-362.

KINMAN, T. (1982) "Raising a child with Down's syndrome," pp. 138-140 in P. Evans (ed.) How a Baby Changed My Life. Wauwatosa, WI: American Baby Books.

KIRKLAND, J. (1983) "Infant crying—problem that won't go away!" Parents' Centre Bulletin 96 (Summer): 15-17.

———F. DEANE, and M. BRENNAN (1983) "About CrySOS, a clinic for people with crying babies." Family Relations 32 (October): 537-543.

KITZINGER, S. (1978) Women as Mothers: How They See Themselves in Different Cultures. New York: Random House.

KLEIN, B. L. (1980) "Families of handicapped children: a personal account." Dimensions: Journal of the Southern Association of Children Under Six 9 (October): 55-58.

KOPP, M. E. (1934) Birth Control in Practice: Analysis of Ten Thousand Case Histories of the Birth Control Research Bureau. New York: McBride.

KOVIT, L. (1972) "Labor is hard work: notes on the social organization of childbirth." Sociological Symposium 8 (Spring): 11-21.

KRANNICH, R. S. (1980) "Abortion in the United States: past, present, and future trends." Family Relations 29 (July): 365-374.

LAMAZE, F. (1956) Painless Childbirth: Psychophrophylactic Method. New York: Harper & Row.

LANGWAY, L., with T. JACKSON, M. ZABARSKY, D. SHIRLEY, and J. WHITMORE (1983) "Bringing up superbaby." Newsweek (April): 62-68.

LaROSSA, R. (1977) Conflict and Power in Marriage: Expecting the First Child. Beverly Hills, CA: Sage.

———(1978) "Negotiating a sexual reality during pregnancy: language and marital politics." Presented at the annual meeting of the Southern Sociological Society, New Orleans (April).

———(1979) "Sex during pregnancy: a symbolic interactionist analysis." Journal of Sex Research 15 (May): 119-128.

———(1983) "The transition to parenthood and the social reality of time." Journal of Marriage and the Family 45 (August): 579-589.

———and M. MULLIGAN LaROSSA (1981) Transition to Parenthood: How Infants Change Families. Beverly Hills, CA: Sage.

LEDERMAN, R. P. (1984) Psychosocial Adaptation in Pregnancy: Assessment of Seven Dimension of Maternal Development. Englewood Cliffs, NJ: Prentice-Hall.

LEIFER, M. (1980) Psychological Effects of Motherhood: A Study of First Pregnancy. New York: Praeger.

LEO, J. and B. KALB (1985) "Bringing Dr. Spock up-to-date: the famed best seller appears in its fifth version." Time (April 8).

LIGHT, S. (1985) "Female infanticide in China." Response to the Victimization of Women: Journal of the Center for Women Policy Studies 8 (Spring): 5-6.

LORBER, J., R. L. COSER, A. S. ROSSI, and N. CHODOROW (1981) "On The Reproduction of Mothering: a methodological debate." Signs: Journal of Women in Culture and Society 6 (Spring): 482-514.

LUCAS, R. and L. I. MILLER (1981) "Evolution of abortion law in North America," pp. 75-120 in J. E. Hodgson (ed.) Abortion and Sterilization: Medical and Social Aspects. London: Academic Press.

LUKER, K. (1984) Abortion and the Politics of Motherhood. Berkeley: University of California Press.

McBRIDE, A. (1982) "The American way of birth," pp. 413-429 in M. A. Kay (ed.) Anthropology of Human Birth. Philadelphia: F. A. Davis.

McCALL, R. M. (1979) Infants. Cambridge, MA: Harvard University Press.

McCAULEY, C. S. (1976) Pregnancy After 35. New York: Dutton.

McCORKEL, R. J. (1964) "Husbands and pregnancy: an exploratory study." M.A. thesis, University of North Carolina.

McWHIRTER, N. (1984) Guinness Book of World Records. New York: Bantam Books.

MELVILLE, K. (1983) Marriage and Family Today. New York: Random House.

MILINAIRE, C. (1971) Birth: Facts and Legends. New York: Crown.

MILLER, M. A. and D. A. BROOTEN (1983) The Childbearing Family: A Nursing Perspective. Boston: Little, Brown.

MILLER, R. S. (1978) "The social construction and reconstruction of physiological events: acquiring the pregnancy identity." Studies in Symbolic Interaction 1: 181-204.

MILLS, C. W. (1959) The Sociological Imagination. London: Oxford University Press.

MOSHER, W. D. and C. A. BACHRACH (1982) "Childlessness in the United States: estimates from the national survey of family growth." Journal of Family Issues 3 (December): 517-543.

MYLES, M. F. (1971) A Textbook for Midwives. Baltimore: Williams & Wilkins.

NASH, A. and J. E. NASH (1979) "Conflicting interpretations of childbirth: the medical and natural perspectives." Urban Life 7 (January): 493-512.

National Center for Health Statistics (1985) "Births, marriages, divorces, and deaths for April 1985." Monthly Vital Statistics Report (DHHS Pub. 85-1120) 34 (July 19): 1-12.

NIHELL, E. (1760) A Treatise on the Art of Midwifery: Setting Forth Various Abuses Therein, Especially as to the Practice with Instruments. London.

OAKLEY, A. (1980). Becoming a Mother. New York: Schocken.

O'CONNELL, M. and C. C. ROGERS (1982) "Differential fertility in the United States: 1976-1980." Family Planning Perspectives 14 (September/October): 281-286.

O'DONNELL, L. (1982) "The social worlds of parents." Marriage and Family Review 5 (Winter): 9-36.

OLSON, L. (1983) Costs of Children. Lexington, MA: D. C. Heath.

ORY, H. W., J. D. FORREST, and R. LINCOLN (1983) Making Choices: Evaluating the Health Risks and Benefits of Birth Control Methods. New York: Alan Guttmacher Institute.

Oxford English Dictionary (1970) London: Oxford University Press.

PARKE, R. D. (1981) Fathers. Cambridge, MA: Harvard University Press.

PECK, E. (1971) The Baby Trap. New York: Pinnacle Books.

———(1977) The Joy of the Only Child. New York: Delacorte.

PEPPERS, L. G. and R. J. KNAPP (1980) Motherhood and Mourning: Perinatal Death. New York: Praeger.

PLECK, J. H. (1983) "Husbands' paid work and family roles: current research issues," pp. 251-333 in H. Lopata and J. H. Pleck (eds.) Research in the Interweave of Social Roles, Vol. 3: Families and Jobs. Greenwich, CT: JAI Press.

POLATNICK, M. (1973) "Why men don't rear children: a power analysis." Berkeley Journal of Sociology 18: 45-86.

PRITCHARD, J. A. (1984) Williams Obstetrics. New York: Appleton-Century-Crofts.

RAYNALDE, T. (1626) The Byrth of Mankind. London.

REDICAN, W. K. (1976) "Adult male-infant interactions in nonhuman primates," pp. 345-385 in M. E. Lamb (ed.) The Role of the Father in Child Development. New York: John Wiley.

REED, J. D. (1982) "The new baby boom." Time 119 (February): 52-58.

ROBERTS, F. B. and B. C. MILLER (1978) "Infant behavior effects on the transition to parenthood." Presented at the annual meeting of Theory Construction and Research Methodology Workshop of the National Council on Family Relations, October.

ROBERTSON, I. (1981) Sociology. New York: Worth.

RORVICK, D. M. and L. B. SHETTLES (1970) Your Baby's Sex: Now You Can Choose. New York: Dodd, Mead.

ROSENGREN, W. R. (1962) "The sick role during pregnancy." Journal of Health and Human Behavior 3 (Fall): 213-218.

ROSSI, A. S. (1968) "Transition to parenthood." Journal of Marriage and the Family 30 (February): 26-39.

———(1977) "A biosocial perspective on parenting." Daedalus 106 (Spring): 1-31.

———(1981) "On the reproduction of mothering: a methodological debate." Signs: Journal of Women in Culture and Society 6 (Spring): 492-500.

———(1984) "Gender and parenthood: American Sociological Association, 1983 presidential address." American Sociological Review 49 (February): 1-19.

ROTHMAN, B. K. (1982) In Labor: Women and Power in the Birthplace. New York: Norton.

ROUSSEAU, J. J. (1762) Emile. Paris: Pleide.

SCANZONI, J. (1979) "Social processes and power in families," pp. 295-316 in W. R. Burr et al. (eds.) Contemporary Theories About the Family, Vol. 1: Research-Based Theories. New York: Free Press.

SCANZONI, L. D. and J. SCANZONI (1981) Men, Women, and Change: A Sociology of Marriage and Family. New York: McGraw-Hill.

SCHUTZ, A. (1971) Collected Papers I: The Problems of Social Reality. The Hague: Martinus Nijhoff.

SCOTT, M. B. and S. M. LYMAN (1968) "Accounts." American Sociological Review 33 (February): 46-62.

SHEEHY, G. (1974) Passages: Predictable Crises of Adult Life. New York: Dutton.

SHERESHEFSKY, P. M. and L. Y. YARROW (1973) Psychological Aspects of a First Pregnancy and Early Postnatal Adaptation. New York: Raven Press.

SHORTER, E. (1975) The Making of the Modern Family. New York: Basic Books.

SKOLNICK, A. S. (1983) The Intimate Environment: Exploring Marriage and the Family. Boston: Little, Brown.

SOREL, N. C. (1984) Ever Since Eve: Personal Reflections on Childbirth. New York: Oxford University Press.

SOSNOWITZ, B. (1984) "Managing parents on neonatal intensive care units." Social Problems 31 (April): 390-402.

STAINTON, M. C. (1985) "The fetus: a growing member of the family." Family Relations 34 (July): 321-326.

STARR, P. (1982) The Social Transformation of American Medicine. New York: Basic Books.

Statistical Abstracts of the United States (1976) Washington, DC: Government Printing Office.
———(1985) Washington, DC: Government Printing Office.
STOKES, R. and J. P. HEWITT (1976) "Aligning actions." American Sociological Review 41 (October): 838-849.
STORER, H. (1868) Criminal Abortion. Boston.
SWEET, J. A. (1982) "Work and fertility," pp. 197-218 in G. L. Fox (ed.) The Childbearing Decision: Fertility Attitudes and Behavior. Beverly Hills, CA: Sage.
TAYLOR, S. E. and E. J. LANGER (1977) "Pregnancy: a social stigma?" Sex Roles 3 (February): 27-35.
THIBAUT, J. W. and H. H. KELLEY (1959) The Social Psychology of Groups. New York: John Wiley.
THOMAS, A. and S. CHESS (1980) The Dynamics of Psychological Development. New York: Brunner/Mazel.
THORNTON, A. and D. FREEDMAN (1983) "The changing American family." Population Bulletin 38 (October).
THURMAN, J. (1982) "Breaking the mother-daughter code: an interview with Nancy Chodorow." Ms. 11 (September): 34-35, 36, 38, 138-139.
TIETZE, C. and S. LEWIT (1981) "Epidemiology of induced abortion," pp. 41-56 in J. E. Jodgson (ed.) Abortion and Sterilization: Medical and Social Aspects. London: Academic Press.
TOLSTOY, L. (1878) Anna Karenina. Available in several translations.
TREBILCOT, J. [ed.] (1983) Mothering: Essays in Feminist Theory. Totowa, NJ: Rowman & Allanheld.
U.S. Bureau of Labor Statistics (1981) Special Labor Force Reports. Washington, DC: Government Printing Office.
VEEVERS, J. E. (1973) "The social meanings of parenthood." Psychiatry 36 (August): 291-310.
———(1980) Childless by Choice. Toronto: Butterworths.
Vital Statistic Rates in the United States, 1940-1960 (1968) Washington, DC: Government Printing Office.
WAITE, L. J., G. W. HAGGSTROM, and D. E. KANOUSE (1985) "Changes in the employment activities of new parents." American Sociological Review 50 (April): 263-272.
WARSHAW, R. (1984) "The American way of birth." Ms. 13 (September): 45-50, 130.
WEBER, M. (1947) The Theory of Social and Economic Organization (T. Parsons, ed.). New York: Oxford University Press.
Webster's New Collegiate Dictionary (1977) Springfield, MA: G. & C. Merriam.
WERTZ, R. W. and D. C. WERTZ (1977) Lying In: A History of Childbirth in America. New York: Schocken.
WETROGAN, S. I. (1983) "Provisional projections of the population of states, by age and sex: 1980 to 2000." Current Population Reports, Series P-25, 937 (August 1983).
WHELAN, E. M. (1975) A Baby? . . . Maybe: A Guide to Making the Most Fateful Decision of Your Life. New York: Bobbs-Merrill.
———(1978) The Pregnancy Experience: The Psychology of Expectant Parenthood. New York: Norton.

WILKIE, J. R. (1981) "The trend toward delayed parenthood." Journal of Marriage and the Family 43 (August): 583-591.

ZERUBAVEL, E. (1979) Patterns of Time in Hospital Life: A Sociological Perspective. Chicago: University of Chicago Press.

———(1981) Hidden Rhythms: Schedules and Calendars in Social Life. Chicago: University of Chicago Press.

Name Index

Subject Index

About the Author

Ralph LaRossa developed a sociological interest in fertility, pregnancy, birth, and infant care when he found that by studying couples soon before or after they became parents he could observe family processes that generally are beyond the researcher's view. His personal interest in these subjects was sparked by the births of his sons, Brian and Adam. A graduate of St. Peter's College, the New School for Social Research, and the University of New Hampshire, he currently is Associate Professor of Sociology at Georgia State University in Atlanta. His previous books include *Conflict and Power in Marriage: Expecting the First Child, Transition to Parenthood: How Infants Change Families* (with Maureen Mulligan LaRossa), and *Family Case Studies: A Sociological Perspective.*

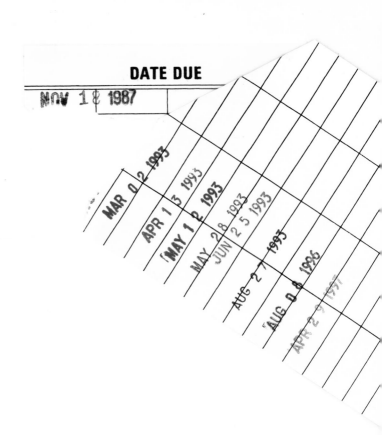